Where Have All the Intellectuals Gone?

Also available from Continuum:

Where Have All the Intellectuals Gone?

Confronting 21st Century Philistinism

Frank Furedi

continuum
LONDON • NEW YORK

Continuum
The Tower Building
11 York Road
London SE1 7NX
www.continuumbooks.com

15 East 26th Street
New York
NY 10010

Hardback edition reprinted 2004, 2005
Paperback edition published 2005

British Library Cataloguing-in-Publication Data
A catalogue record for this book is available from the British Library.

ISBN: 0-8264-6769-5 (hardback)
ISBN: 0-8264-8821-8 (paperback)

Typeset by BookEns Ltd, Royston, Herts.
Printed and bound in Great Britain

Contents

Preface   vii

Introduction: A Personal Journey Through the Land of
the Philistines   1

1   Devaluing the Intellect   25

2   Trivial Pursuits   50

3   Dumbing Down   72

4   Social Engineering   92

5   The Culture of Flattery   114

6   Treating People as Children   137

Bibliography   157

Index   162

Preface

For some time now I have been disturbed by the profound sense of intellectual disorientation that appears to afflict many of our cultural institutions, universities and schools. The public deserves a high quality of intellectual debate from our cultural institutions and, as an audience with infinite potential, should command far greater respect. This book is written for the many intelligent men and women who aspire to a more challenging intellectual and cultural life.

The ideas presented in *Where Have All the Intellectuals Gone?* were developed through a protracted conversation with friends and colleagues. The steady stream of correspondence that I received in response to my articles on the university in *The Times Higher Education Supplement* helped convince me that many others shared my concerns. Discussions with friends in the United States suggested that institutional dumbing down was not merely a British problem. An important conference on the Public Intellectual organized by the Institute of Ideas in London during the summer of 2003 helped reorient this study towards an exploration of the wider question of cultural politics.

Throughout the course of writing this book I received constant feedback and criticism from Josie Appleton. For better or worse, she is responsible for the direction of many of my arguments. I also gained many insights from the input made by two Institute of Ideas stalwarts, Tiffany Jenkins and Claire Fox. My colleague Professor Mary Evans, who was completing her *Death of the University* has helped share the pain. Jenny Bristow helped to turn the manuscript into a more readable text. I am grateful to Anthony Haynes my editor at Continuum, for his generous support throughout all stages of this project.

Introduction

A Personal Journey through the Land of the Philistines

Philistine: A person deficient in liberal culture; one whose interests are material and commonplace.[1]

Unexpected circumstances provoked me to write this book. In May 2001 I wrote an article 'What is university for now?' for *The Sunday Times*, in which I raised some of my concerns about the direction of the British university. The article focused on the relative absence of intellectual stimulation and challenge on contemporary campuses. I related stories told to me by undergraduates who were profoundly bored by their university experience, and pointed out that in many cases, students could spend an entire year at university without reading a whole book.

A day after the publication of this article, I received an irate email from a senior university manager. This person was clearly incensed by my comments and accused me of 'deliberately' confusing the issues. After reading the first few angry lines I was expecting him to accuse me of fabricating my claim that undergraduates could spend a year without reading a book – but that was not the focus of his objection. He had no problem with the estrangement of undergraduates from the world of books; rather, he was angry about my arrogant assumption that books should have a privileged status in higher education. 'The tone of

[1] The Shorter Oxford Dictionary (1963), p. 1487.

the article was to suggest that you can dismiss as undemanding any programme in which students do not read "whole books"', he complained. As far as he was concerned, the book has become an optional extra resource for the present-day undergraduate.

In the months that followed this exchange, his quotation marks around 'whole books' continued to prey on my thoughts. I had anticipated a measure of hostility to the article but I did not expect a leading academic manager to treat the study of books in such a cavalier manner. Until this email exchange, I believed that despite differences over pedagogy and scholarship, the higher education establishment shared some of my misgivings and was likely to feel uncomfortable, if not embarrassed, by the evident banalization of university life. I took the view that the marginalization of intellectual passion in higher education was the unintended consequence of a new ethos of managerialism that dominates intellectual and cultural life, and was not expecting the upfront celebration of philistinism, as exemplified by my correspondent's in-your-face disparagement of studying books.

Yet I did not have to look very hard to realize that this was not the eccentric response of a maverick university administrator. Far from being defensive, the current cultural elite regards any preoccupation with the routinization of intellectual life as an object worthy of its collective scorn. Meanwhile, the behaviour of this elite is dictated by instrumentalism – an ethos that values art, culture and education insofar as they serve as instruments for serving a wider practical purpose.

Individual scholars pursuing their passionate interests increasingly risk labels such as 'irrelevant', 'elitist', 'out-of-touch' and 'marginal'. Scholarship, the pursuit of excellence and truth, is frequently represented as a bizarre, self-indulgent and irrelevant pursuit. 'A bit dodgy' is how Charles Clarke, the British Secretary of State for Education, has described the idea of education for its own sake, while asserting that his government has no interest in supporting 'the medieval concept of a community of scholars seeking truth'. Clarke's depiction of the aspiration for knowledge as an irrelevant form of medieval prejudice is testimony to the philistine ethos that informs much of educational and cultural policy today.

Such attitudes are not confined to British society or to politicians of any particular party. Clarke's Tory predecessors were no less convinced that the main purpose of education was to act as engines of economic growth. Even at the best of times, the pursuit of ideas for their own sake was an ideal that was rarely realized in practice. But at least it was an ideal that was outwardly valued by significant sections of society. Today, it is increasingly at odds with the instrumentalist ethos of global culture. 'There is a growing perception, both among students and in the university, that the humanities and languages are unnecessary indulgences', observed Vrinda Nabar, former head of the English Literature department of Mumbai University in India.[2] So too in the United States. Between 1970 and 1995, the number of foreign language majors in universities declined by 37 per cent.

Of course philistine attitudes towards education, art and culture are not a peculiarly novel development. Some of the great nineteenth-century thinkers – Mathew Arnold, Nietzsche, Goethe, Marx – were sensitive to the way in which the impersonal force of the market impinged on the development of art and culture. However, today, the influence of philistinism is not contingent on the pragmatic routines demanded by economic realities. Philistine influences are not only directed at education and culture from the outside – they have become institutionalized at the highest level of policy-making. There is a new breed of university managers, museum and gallery directors and 'know-

[2]   See Shabnam Minwalla 'Commerce is the mantra of the moment in city colleges', *Education Times*, September 2003. *www.educationtimes.com/arts.htm*

ledge' entrepreneurs who regard the content of culture and ideas with indifference. Their concern is to use culture to achieve an objective that is quite separate from its inner content.

The contempt that Charles Clarke displayed towards the idea of 'scholars seeking truth' expresses the temper of our times. Such cynical attitudes are underpinned by a consensus that regards the possibility of discovering the truth with scepticism. In previous times, the claim to pursue the truth sometimes covered up a variety of misdeeds. What passed for the truth were sometimes ideologies designed to serve the purposes of vested interests. But at least truth was valued for its own sake. For Aristotle, truth was the object of science: 'Philosophy is the science which considers truth.' For Albert Einstein, 'the search for truth' was 'more precious than its possession'. Rosa Luxemburg was equally passionate about the search for the truth. 'But this much I know, that it is our duty, if we desire to teach truth, to teach it wholly or not at all, to teach it clearly and bluntly, unenigmatically, unreservedly, inspired with full confidence in its powers', she told her audience. It is this passionate search for the truth that has inspired generations of thinkers during the era of modernity.

Unfortunately, contemporary culture regards the truth as a subject worthy of fiction rather than of intellectual pursuit. It is frequently argued that there is no such thing as the truth. Instead of the truth, people are exhorted to accept different opinions as representing many truths. Michel Foucault's claim that there is 'no truly universal truth' has gained widespread influence in academic circles. Truth is rarely represented as an objective fact; it is frequently portrayed as the product of subjective insight, which is in competition with other equally valid perspectives. Relativism – a perspective that contends that conceptions of truth and moral values are not absolute but are relative to the persons or groups holding them – has acquired a commanding influence over cultural life. The view that truth is in the eye of the beholder has had a significant impact on the workings of educational and cultural institutions. If the truth is relegated to the status of subjective outlook and interpretation, it ceases to be a subject of fundamental importance. It is certainly not a matter of life and death. Nor can its discovery serve as the principal justification of any significant institution. Once truth is interpreted as a dubious claim in competition with many others, it ceases to play a key role in a society's cultural life.

The demotion of the status of the truth has had significant impact on contemporary cultural life. Classical insights into the status of art – 'beauty is truth and truth is beauty' – appear inconsistent with an ethos that can only conceive of truth in the plural form. Intellectual life too must also undergo serious modification. As one important study of the role of the university remarked, 'liberal higher education has rested on the assumption that objective knowledge and truth are attainable' – before adding that 'this assumption has recently been put in doubt with modern developments in philosophy, such as relativism, critical theory and post-structuralism'. According to Ron Barnett, the author of this study, 'this amounts to an epistemological undermining of higher education'.[3] At the very least, the meaning of higher education becomes transformed once its claim to providing a pathway to the truth has been undermined.

The cavalier orientation towards the truth is also evident in relation to the wider manifestations of cultural life. The best that society can offer is now far from evident. Culture with a capital C has given way to cultures, and any claim to authority or special status is treated with derision. The conventional distinction between high and low culture makes little sense in an environment where truth has such an elusive quality. The former British Culture Secretary, Chris Smith, echoed this sentiment when he declared that the distinction between 'high

[3]   Barnett (1990), p. X.

culture' and 'low culture' is a misleading one and that 'George Benjamin and Noel Gallagher are both musicians of the first rank'.

Throughout the human experience culture authority has rested on the claim to represent truth. Today such sentiments tend to be treated with scepticism. Indeed, such claims are frequently castigated as elitist, and the aspiration to excellence and high standards is dismissed as a foolish lament for a golden age. Elitism, which once meant justifying a monopoly of economic, cultural and political power through the self-conscious disparagement of the people, has been redefined as the act of valuing certain aspects of culture above others. It is striking that such views tend to influence almost the entire spectrum of opinion. It is not simply the so-called cultural left that dismisses objective knowledge – the cultural elites themselves are reluctant to affirm any transcendental cultural values and truths. Instead of affirming their authority, the cultural elites appear more interested in appearing relevant, accessible and in touch with popular opinion.

Knowledge without meaning

It is paradoxical that cynicism about objective knowledge coincides with the widely held view that we live in a Knowledge Society in which it is often observed that 'knowledge is power'. Commentators frequently declare the need to respond to the demands of a Knowledge Economy, while the expansion of higher education and other cultural initiatives are justified on the grounds that they are needed for the development of a Knowledge Society. Universities and other educational institutions are regularly promoted on the grounds that they are vital for economic progress. In July 2003, the Bank of England's monetary policy committee declared that Cambridge and Oxford universities play a 'vital role in the United Kingdom economy'.[4] In the US, successive administrations have treated knowledge as a weapon vital to the nation's security.

Precisely at a time when the intellectual authority of knowledge is widely questioned, education and learning have assumed an unprecedented significance. The public is continually exhorted to become lifelong learners and to acquire new knowledge. Business and public institutions constantly avow their commitment to expanding their knowledge base. Knowledge has become a brand embraced by virtually every significant institution. But, unfortunately, the contemporary imagination endows knowledge with a superficial, almost banal, character. Often knowledge is conceptualized as a ready-made digestible product that can be 'delivered', 'transmitted', 'marketed' and 'consumed'. Mary Evans likens the academic institution to the catering industry where students receive the correct 'portion'. The transformation of knowledge into a product deprives it of any intrinsic value or meaning, and the knowledge that is peddled by the merchants of the Knowledge Economy is in fact a mundane caricature of itself. Why? Because without a relationship to Truth, knowledge has no intrinsic meaning. It becomes an abstract insight that is more likely to be transmitted than valued, and can be recycled in its most mundane form.

When knowledge is regarded as a product, its relationship to its own cultural and intellectual origin becomes indistinct. Knowledge is increasingly seen as the product of a technical process rather than of human intellectual work. For this reason, the postmodernist Jean-François Lyotard could claim the imminent 'death of the professor'. Lyotard noted that a professor is 'no more competent than memory bank networks in transmitting established knowledge'.[5] At a time when it has

---

4   See 'Oxbridge told to modernise', BBC News: 15 July 2003.
5   Lyotard (1984), p. 53.

become quiet fashionable to declare the 'death of the author', the 'death of the book' or the 'death of the subject', the relationship between knowledge and its intellectual origin becomes less and less clear.

The cult of the banal

During the past two centuries, the authority of intellectuals was underwritten by the belief that the pursuit of knowledge and truth merited the affirmation of society. This belief endowed intellectual work with a unique significance and provided intellectuals with an intense sense of purpose towards their mission. Indeed within the humanist tradition, intellectual and contemplative activity was represented as the highest form of human endeavour, and it was often claimed that it was this endeavour that distinguished the human from the animal.

Today, this lofty image of the intellectual appears inconsistent with the way that society regards the pursuit of knowledge. Scepticism about the possibility of objective knowledge has not only had an impact on the institution of higher education, it also has had a significant influence on intellectual life in general. If there is nothing special about knowledge, its pursuit becomes a meaningless ritual. In turn, the diminishing significance attached to knowledge has important implications for how intellectuals are regarded and how they regard themselves. In previous times, the heroic self-image of the intellectual with its extravagant pretensions was rightly mocked by satirists and critics – George Orwell, for example, gave a trenchant critique of his intellectual contemporaries. Yet despite his criticism of intellectual slothfulness, Orwell retained his belief that ideas had the power to help create a better world. Often the very force of the criticism directed at intellectuals represented an acknowledgement of the force of ideas. In the twenty-first century, by contrast, the heroic image of the classical intellectual has given way to a more down-to-earth pragmatic person, whose job is not a particularly important one. This devaluation of the role of the intellectual is intimately linked to current attitudes towards knowledge. If the search for knowledge no longer excites the cultural imagination, it is inevitable that the status of the intellectual will also cease to possess its special unique qualities.

A depressingly pedestrian account of intellectual life is regularly transmitted in discussions on this subject. The classical ideal of the search for truth associated with the intellectual has given way to one in which the pursuit of ideas is bereft of any lofty purpose. A sceptical attitude towards the role of the intellectual is not confined to the stereotypical know-nothing populist philistine. Many intellectuals have internalized the pragmatism associated with their activities, and insist that there is nothing special that defines them. This complacent attitude towards the role of the intellectual also influences academic writing on the subject. 'Perhaps it's time that someone wrote an essay entitled "Intellectuals are ordinary"', observed the Cambridge University historian Stefan Collini. Collini's aspiration to demystify the role of the intellectual very much reflects a culture that finds it difficult to endow the pursuit of ideas with very much meaning. Collini explains what he means by 'ordinary':

'Ordinary' in the sense that they are indeed part of the cultural landscape of all complex societies; ordinary in the sense that it is neither unthinkable nor shocking to recognize that the noun 'intellectual' might regularly be applied to some of one's friends or one's colleagues or even, in some circumstances, oneself; and above all, ordinary in the sense that carrying on the activities characteristic of intellectuals should not be seen as exceptionally heroic or exceptionally difficult or exceptionally glamorous or – and I realize here I particularly lay myself open to misunderstanding – even

exceptionally important. Important, yes, but not exceptionally important.[6]

It could be argued that there is always a case for demystifying the
sacred aura that often surrounded intellectual work. Nowadays,
however, such a project amounts to little more than kicking
against an open door. The work of today's intellectual is rarely
represented as 'exceptionally heroic', and rendering intellectual
work banal simply reinforces the low expectations that surrounds
intellectual and cultural life.

There is little doubt that intellectuals can be pompous,
arrogant and full of hot air. That is why their pretensions have
often been the target of people's humour and scorn. But such
defects of character notwithstanding, the work of the intellectual
is very important. Without a mission, a project or a desire to
uphold and promote knowledge with a capital K, intellectuals
must of course feel uneasy and constrained; and in such
circumstances the loss of authority, underwritten by engagement
with the pursuit of the truth, must have a major impact on
intellectual life. Unfortunately, these circumstances only help
breed yet more complacency and conformism.

The sociology of dumbing down

At a time when hundreds of undistinguished European towns and
cities fiercely compete with one another to win the title of 'city of
culture', it may appear mean-spirited to write about the rise of
philistinism. Cultural events and festivals are mushrooming
throughout the United States and the rest of the Western world,
and every sleepy town seems to possess a museum or at least a
heritage centre. The claim that society is dumbing down is angrily

---

[6] See Stefan Collini ' "Every fruit juice drinker, nudist, sandal wearer ...".
Intellectuals as Other People' in Small (2002), p. 221.

dismissed by defenders of the cultural status quo, who promote what they perceive as a thriving knowledge ecology. Inevitably they point to the growth in the numbers of books published, the increase in the number of bookshops, the thriving network of book clubs or the large numbers of people attending concerts, art galleries and museums. According to one American observer:

> Externally after all, the life of the mind has seldom seemed healthier in America than it does right now. Magazines, newspaper sections, and Web sites dedicated to the doings of scholars, publishers, and writers have proliferated in the last ten years or so. In college and university towns across America, traditional and cutting-edge forms of cultural life flourish side by side. Readings, debates, and poetry slams draw hundreds. Even after college, intellectual life goes on.[7]

Education has certainly acquired a formidable influence over society. More and more people are participating in higher education. And it seems that people's involvement in education never stops. Everybody appears to be getting some kind of workplace training, or taking a pause while they are retraining. People in their forties are returning to university, or entering for the first time. We are all supposed to be lifelong learners and thousands of institutions exist to cater to every one of our knowledge needs. There is little doubt that we take education and culture seriously. We don't live in a Dark Age where it is impossible to find stimulating and challenging literature. We continue to innovate – sometimes individual artists produce magnificent art, and some intellectuals continue to develop important ideas in the humanities, social and natural sciences.

Cultural pessimists are often not able to refute the establishment's claim that we live in a flourishing knowledge society.

---

[7] Anthony Grafton, 'The Public Intellectual and the American University', *American Scholar*, Autumn 2001.

They point to the rise of reality television at the expense of quality drama and factual programming, the growth of self-indulgent opinion columns in newspapers at the expense of thoughtful news analysis, and the steady erosion of standards at all levels of education. Such criticisms are not without foundation. But not every new project is a Millennium Dome – a testimony to cultural illiteracy. We also have the Wallace Collection or the Guggenheim Museum in Bilbao. Important innovations and institutions able to promote standards of excellence have always been a rarity. So what has changed?

The reason why the metaphor of dumbing down captures the temper of our times has little to do with the current level of cultural, artistic or educational standards. Dumbing down is fuelled by powerful forces that treat knowledge and culture as merely the means for the realization of a wider and higher objective. It is an orientation that is defined by a dogmatic commitment to instrumentalism. Such an orientation is not new – the tension between the demands of the market and economic calculation, and the pursuit of ideas or art for their own sake, has been a recurring theme in cultural debates for over two centuries. Throughout this time, artistic and intellectual endeavour has been seen as driven by interests that directly contradict the instrumentalist ethos of the market. The tension between the two was clearly formulated by Talcott Parsons, probably the most influential American sociologist of the twentieth century: 'The professional man is not thought of as engaging in the pursuit of his personal profit, but in performing services to his clients, or to impersonal values like the advancement of science.'[8]

The age-old tension between economic calculation, and a commitment to impersonal and non-instrumental values such as the advancement of knowledge and science, has meant that the intellectual and the artist were historically in a state of creative

---

[8]   Parsons (1954), p. 186.

conflict with the rest of society. Indeed, what was distinct and valued about artistic and intellectual activity was precisely that it was not directly dominated by an instrumental ethos. Artists and intellectuals did not set out to produce what the customer wanted, but sought to realize a loftier objective. In practice the line that divided self-interest from the disinterested pursuit of knowledge was often breached, but nevertheless the rhetoric of pursuing ideas for their own sake informed the project of the intellectual.

It is worth noting that even societies that wholeheartedly subscribed to the virtues of the market, for example the United States and Britain, continued to affirm values associated with intellectual and artistic endeavour. It was recognized that such efforts were valuable in their own right rather than because they had a high price tag attached to them. For their part – with greater or lesser effectiveness – artists and intellectuals defended their efforts because they were convinced that what they were doing was valuable in its own right.

It is only in recent times that the instrumentalist ethos has managed to dominate the way society perceives its artistic and intellectual activities. There are a number of interconnected and mutually reinforcing influences that account for this development, some of which will be further explored in the following chapters. One reason for this development is the cumulative impact of Western society's disenchantment with the legacy of the Enlightenment. As noted previously, if knowledge and the pursuit of the truth can no longer claim to make a big difference, the authority of the intellectual becomes discounted. In such circumstances the claims to intellectual autonomy, artistic integrity or disinterested professionalism become highly suspect. Once the special status that the Enlightenment tradition assigned to knowledge becomes discredited, it becomes difficult to endow intellectual and artistic activity with any special and intrinsic meaning. Such activities are represented as careers that are not

qualitatively different from other occupations. In such circumstances knowledge and art are not likely to be valued for
themselves, but because of their usefulness for society.

If knowledge and art lack any inner meaning, the reaffirmation
that they ought to be valued for their own sake can appear as a
form of special pleading. The demand to uphold certain
intellectual or artistic standards also appears inconsistent with
the absence of any agreed criteria for measuring those achievements. In any case it is not the content of ideas and art that are
valued but their utility. Consequently, how knowledge and art
are regarded is determined, not by criteria that are internal to
themselves, but by their utility for some other purpose. In such
circumstances knowledge and art serve as instruments of
economic advance, social engineering, giving communities an
identity, or providing therapy for the individual. The triumph of
this instrumentalist approach is underwritten by the inability of
contemporary society to endow intellectual and artistic work
with meaning. So while we still produce good art and books, we
find it difficult to value them in their own terms.

Why should the triumph of instrumentalism lead to dumbing
down? If we cannot value intellectual and cultural achievements
in their own terms, it becomes difficult to discriminate between
them. Claims to excellence sound self-serving if not mendacious,
and are frequently dismissed as a despicable attempt by an elite to
protect its privileges. That is why the term 'standards' has
acquired the connotation of privilege and elitism – to the extent
that in many circumstances, the insistence on upholding a
particular standard is represented as a form of institutionalized
discrimination.

Debates about educational standards are invariably terminated
with the argument that those who demand to uphold past
practices are indifferent to meeting the needs of students today.
The cultural elite does not so much call for the abandonment of
the standard of excellence. Rather, it subordinates the main-

tenance of such standards to the imperative of utility. It is the priority assigned to the utility of art and education over its inner content that continually fuels the tendency towards dumbing down. Once the inner content of art and knowledge ceases to have a socially accepted meaning, then standards become negotiable, and easily subordinated to pragmatic and instrumentalist concerns. In her first speech as Minister of State of the Arts at the Cheltenham Literature Festival, Baroness Tessa Blackstone asked: 'Can the arts be more than just frivolous, trivial, irrelevant?' Her answer was yes, but only if they can be used for purposes other than aesthetic ones. For Blackstone the arts are important because apparently they improve employability, eradicate inequality and help prevent crime. '[I have] no doubt that the arts can contribute to improving health outcomes', she added.

In previous times the dumbing down of culture was classically the result of the operation of the market on intellectual life. Back in the 1930s, F. R. Leavis pointed the finger at the commercial imperative for the massification of culture. The commercial imperative is no less significant today than in the past. But today it is not market forces that are primarily responsible for the process of dumbing down. Rather, it is a direct consequence of public policy that promotes the politics of inclusion at any cost. Why this should be the case will be explored in Chapter 5.

Negotiating standards

In the numerous controversies that surround standards, be they about education, art, speech or political life, not even the most vulgar cultural entrepreneur demands abandoning standards of excellence. Instead, those who sneer at the word 'standards' believe that there are many different modes of defining and affirming excellence. The so-called Culture Wars in the US and the incessant debate over educational standards in the UK are symptomatic of a climate where competitive claims-making influences the representation of standards. A standard with a capital S is inconsistent with the mood of contemporary culture. Any claim that privileges a particular art form, way of speaking, or educational achievement, is dismissed on the grounds that they possess no special merit over and above those achieved in different circumstances by other people and other cultures. Moreover, the act of upholding a standard in order to make judgements of value is sometimes depicted as an act of symbolic violence against people from a different cultural background. According to one such account: 'excellence is an intellectual, cultural and social construction that not only represents social inequalities through its reflective practices, but as well, arbitrariness as a characteristic of its construction'.[9]

The flourishing of relativist critiques of truth and knowledge has been facilitated by the reluctance of the contemporary cultural elite to uphold and clearly define standards. It has no fundamental principles to uphold and accepts no responsibility for forging a consensus around what ought to constitute the achievement of excellence. Since the very notion of a standard is depicted as elitist, it feels uneasy about promoting clearly defined ideals. It is happy to turn an institution like the BBC into an all-purpose medium that self-consciously professes to be flexible on this subject. Individuals within the cultural elites may have a clear view on the subject of what standards society ought to aspire to achieve, but as a collective entity they experience standards as a potential source of conflict and controversy. Consequently the cultural elite regards the maintenance of standards as at best a mixed blessing and at worst an obstacle to avoid.

The growing scepticism towards standards is most striking in discussions about assessing achievement. It is not unusual to hear

---

[9]   Romero, A. (1998), 'Educational change and discourse communities: representing change in post modern times', *Curriculum Studies* 6, p. 53.

members of the UK educational establishment explain that the examination system is elitist and discriminates against the intellectual skill acquired by working-class people. In a similar way, museums, galleries and even libraries have been criticized for not valuing the skills of people from different backgrounds. From a relativistic perspective, the very attempt to measure achievement according to common standards is likely to be discriminatory, if not oppressive.

Different cultures and experiences have a lot to contribute to the development of human civilization. But the targeting of standards has little to do with an enlightened appreciation of human culture. Hostility towards a Standard with a capital S is often fuelled by the belief that the effort and expectation that it embodies is beyond the capacity of most people. This sentiment is most striking in education, where there are desperate attempts made to ensure that people achieve some kind of a qualification. As a result standards are continuously reconfigured to ensure that students succeed. Grade inflation and the devaluation of diplomas and degrees only increase the appetite for further fiddling with the mode of assessment. Policy-makers no longer pretend to endow standards with any objective existence – they have simply become the tools of social policy. Some advocates of this approach even go so far as to identify such 'inclusive' policies as a form of best practice. 'We contend that being inclusive is one measure of educational excellence' argue advocates of 'inclusive education'.[10]

Today's manipulative attitude towards standards is in part a product of disappointment with the experience of reform in education, culture and social policy. Attempts to provide equal opportunities to all sections of society have not led to the

[10] Nunan, T., Rigmor, George and McCausland, H. (2000), 'Inclusive education in universities: why it is important and how it might be achieved', *International Journal of Inclusive Education* 4(1), p. 70.

elimination of privilege serving as a passport to success. As a result there is widespread unease about the relationship between effort and achievement. Instead of exploring why mobility based on merit has had only a limited success, the tendency is to write off the meritocratic ideal altogether. Pessimism now shapes contemporary views towards the meritocratic ideal, which tends to be denounced as an apology for the success of those with accumulated privilege while others are consigned to a life of failure.

From meritocracy to mediocracy

The most striking manifestation of a cavalier approach towards aspiring to standards of excellence is a growing tendency to dismiss the meritocratic ideal as an impossible con trick. The meritocratic ideal claimed that through the provision of equality of opportunity, the most able individuals would be able to rise to the top of society. The principle of merit would replace reliance of inheritance and family ties as the main instrument of social advance. The meritocratic ideal did not simply provide a linkage between individual effort and success – it also held out the promise of cumulative development through harnessing the provision of equality of opportunity to the achievement of the highest standards. As such, it can also be understood as an attempt to achieve the highest possible cultural standards through giving a free rein to the flourishing of merit.

There are considerable obstacles to people of different backgrounds having an opportunity to exercise their talents and realize their potential. Privilege and wealth provide the new generation with unfair advantage and make it difficult for others to rise to the top. But despite all the obstacles that stood in the way of its realization, it was felt that the meritocratic ideal was worth fighting for. Today, by contrast, there is a sharp decline in the enthusiasm for the principle of promoting achievement through merit. The ideal of merit, like that of a standard, is often portrayed as an act of deception designed by a dishonest elite in order to fool the people.

A powerful school of thought used to believe that the democratization of education and culture is compatible with the maintenance, indeed the rise, of standards. Yet in recent years, this idea has taken a severe knock. Those disposed towards traditional elitist ideals have always believed that the democratization of education and culture was inconsistent with the maintenance of excellence in intellectual life. Today, this current of opinion still persists, but is rarely expressed in open form. In today's political climate the democratization of education and culture is rarely questioned. Almost every institution possesses a mission statement that sets out the widening of participation as one of its principal objectives. It is not the democratization of culture that is interrogated today, but the attempt to preserve or raise educational or cultural standards. And the reason why the desirability of upholding standards is put to question by advocates of widening participation is because they, like the traditional elitists, genuinely do not believe that the democratization of cultural life can be reconciled with standards of excellence.

In a roundabout way, today's cultural leaders accept the traditional elitist diagnosis but draw radically different conclusions. They want democracy but are prepared to be flexible about the maintenance of standards. While they may not come out and say this, cultural leaders claim that the project of maintaining high standards is elitist and inherently anti-democratic. That is why arguments that seek to promote excellence in art, culture and education are frequently dismissed as an elitist attempt to turn the clock back to the days when only a tiny minority could have access to cultural capital.

The aim of this book is to question the pessimistic assumption that portrays popular participation as inconsistent with the maintenance of standards of excellence. I argue that the internalization of this perspective by today's cultural elite has led to a flourishing of philistinism and an unhealthy instrument-alism towards intellectual life; and that, furthermore, participa-tion without the maintenance of standards represents a fraud inflicted on millions of people, which disorients society from realizing its potential in the century ahead. This book is devoted to promoting the project of developing society's intellectual and cultural life through the development of an educated public.

The merit of merit

One of the central arguments advanced against the maintenance of standards of excellence is that this is an elitist project that will exclude the vast majority from participating in institutions of culture. This pessimistic conclusion is based on the premise that the public lacks the resources to benefit from demanding forms of cultural and educational experience. As a result, it is argued that standards and expectations will have to change in order to facilitate widening participation. This sceptical assessment of people's abilities has encouraged a mood of hostility towards the idea of rewarding people according to their merit.

Suspicion of standards and merit go hand in hand. It is worth noting that Michael Young's *The Rise of the Meritocracy* (1958), a classical attack on the meritocratic ideal, caricatures a meritocratic statement as: 'no longer is it so necessary to debase standards by attempting to extend a higher civilization to the children of the lower classes'. This association of reactionary elitism with concern about people debasing standards has become part of the collective wisdom of the cultural elite. That is why proposals to select individuals based on merit, the testing of children and adolescents, or the making of judgements of value about art, are often criticized as unfair and elitist.

In economic life, the anti-meritocratic consensus is particularly concerned with the potential for widening economic inequality fuelled by the attitude 'winner takes all'. In relation to wider cultural life, anti-meritocratic sentiment is focused on a preoccupation with failure and the need to immunize people from regarding themselves as failures. 'Every selection of one is a rejection of the many', warns Michael Young's anti-hero.[11] Quarantining the public from a sense of rejection is right at the top of the mission statement of the anti-meritocratic movement.

Of course the meritocratic ideal is rarely realized in practice. Intellectual and cultural life is riddled with discrimination and inequalities. Although many outward forms of discrimination have been eliminated, we are far from achieving a world where individuals can compete on a level playing field. The accident of birth still exercises a decisive role in determining people's life chances. But does the failure to realize the meritocratic ideal represent an argument against it? Or does it, as I believe, represent an argument for reflecting on what went wrong, in order to formulate policies that can eliminate the obstacles that prevent the exercise of individual abilities? Critics of meritocracy in intellectual and cultural life are not seriously engaged with this question. Their main concern is with preventing people from regarding themselves as failures, and this has great influence over policy-makers and the contemporary educational and cultural establishment. As I will argue, it is not so much a democratic impulse that fuels the contemporary rejection of meritocracy, but a therapeutic concern with avoiding feelings of rejection within the wider public.

To put it bluntly, many critics of meritocracy believe that meritocracy leads to mental illness. Testing and selection are said to breed failure and rejection, which in turn are held responsible for the lowering of people's self-esteem. The American social critic

[11] See Young (1961), p. 15.

Christopher Lasch argued that meritocracy has led to an 'obsessive concern' with self-esteem. He claimed that the new therapies 'seek to counter the oppressive sense of failure in those who fail to climb the educational ladder even while they leave intact the existing structure of elite recruitment – the acquisition of educational credentials.[12] There is little doubt that a mood of failure has led to the flourishing of new therapies. However, how individuals feel about themselves, how they engage with the experience of disappointment and the pressures of everyday life, is not reducible to the workings of meritocracy. Such sentiments are the product of wider social and cultural influences. If people feel rejected or lack self-respect it may well be because they are not sure where they belong or how they fit into the wider scheme of things. People can live with disappointment if they have the cultural resources that allow them to make sense of the world. What they need is not to be protected from the sense of failure, but provided with an opportunity to gain insights into their lives through exploring the very best that our culture has to offer. Rewarding merit implies treating people as adults, whereas magicking away the sense of failure is motivated by the desire to treat them as children.

The purpose of the book

This book is not a lament for a lost golden age of intellectual life, when people were smarter, the public received a higher standard of education and creativity, and a more dynamic culture prevailed. We have not turned into simpletons. There are lots of impressive works of art and science and we continue to make remarkable discoveries. In any case, whatever happened in the past is of little help in solving the challenges that we face today.

---

[12] Christopher Lasch, 'Revolt of the Elites', *Harper's Magazine*, November 1994.

In every era, society is confronted with new problems and opportunities. The aim of this book is to question how we are currently going about developing ideas, educating people and creating a new public.

Unfortunately, the debates about education, culture and the arts are dominated by two sides that both convey patronizing anti-democratic sentiments towards the human subject. There is a small minority of opinion that continues to argue that the democratization of intellectual and cultural life will inevitably lead to the decline of standards. From the standpoint of an oligarchical defence of high culture, any attempt to involve the public must lead to the triumph of a lower form of mass culture. Today, very few people are prepared to argue an unambiguous and forthright defence of such an elitist outlook. The dominant side of the debate is outwardly and self-consciously anti-elitist. It continually applauds mass participation, public dialogue and the inclusion of all voices. However, it has little faith in the ability of the public to use and benefit from the best that culture has to offer. Like the traditional elitist perspective, it believes that the people lack the capacity to benefit from standards of excellence. But instead of following the path of the old conservative elites, the new conservative imagination makes no attempt to exclude. Its objective is to transform intellectual and cultural life in order to make it hospitable for a public that cannot be expected to engage with the best. This philistine agenda patronizes the public and treats people like children that need to be protected from more disturbing cultural and intellectual challenges.

The aim of this book is to question both the anti-democratic and patronizing underpinning of contemporary education and cultural politics. Such politics not only restrain intellectual and cultural creativity – they also infantilize the public and lower its expectations. I embrace any attempt to provide the public with opportunities to engage in intellectual exploration. But I decry the paternalistic project of feeding the public with easily digestible portions of knowledge and culture. Inclusion and participation for their own sake has little merit. Flattering people – be they schoolchildren, university students, the audience in a museum – serves only the imperative of social engineering. This book argues that a precondition for expanding genuine public engagement is the provision of standards equivalent to the best that society has to offer.

Dumbing down is not an esoteric issue that concerns only academics, artists and intellectuals. The prevailing level of education, culture and intellectual debate is important for the flourishing of a democratic ethos. Intellectuals in different guises play a crucial role in initiating dialogue and engaging the curiosity and passion of the public. Today that engagement is conspicuously feeble. Unsurprisingly, the cultural elites' cynicism towards knowledge and truth has been transmitted to the people through educational and cultural institutions and the media. Apathy and social disengagement are symptoms of a culture that tends to equate debate with the banal exchange of technical opinions. Because all of this really matters, a culture war against the philistines is long overdue.

1 Devaluing the Intellect

One of the most striking manifestations of the banalization of cultural life is the transformation of the intellectual into a uniquely insignificant figure. Even in France, the supposed home of intellectuals, they appear to lead a life of cultural irrelevance. As an American commentator observed, compared to a figure such as Jean-Paul Sartre, 'Today's French intellectuals look like puny technocrats'.[1]

Intellectuals reflect their culture and the temper of their time. The role they play and the influence that they are able to wield has fluctuated over the past three centuries. This is not the first time that the intellectual is seen to have a feeble presence in society. During the 1950s, at the height of the Cold War, many leading pro-Western thinkers, especially in the United States, were concerned about the exhaustion of intellectual life. Apathy and mental fatigue appeared to afflict those involved in intellectual work. Even the media joined in the discussion and attempted to galvanize into action what it saw as a hibernating intelligentsia. According to one account:

> Throughout the 1950s, magazines and newspapers berated the young as members of a 'silent generation' – politically apathetic, intellectually passive, caring less for social causes, than for economic security, preoccupied with private lives.[2]

---

[1]   Jim Holt, 'Jean-Paul Sartre: Brilliant Philosopher or Totalitarian Apologist?', *Slate*: 22 September 2003.

[2]   Pells (1985), p. 201.

Although superficially this description of events appears to capture the mood of our era, it is important to note that the influence of the intellectual even of the 1950s' 'silent generation' was far greater than in our times. Although it is difficult to measure or compare such influence, it is possible to point to a number of important differences between the periods. The influence of intellectuals on political life, particularly on the left wing of politics, stands in marked contrast to the situation today. And yet, the very public concern with the relative absence of the voice of the intellectual was a testimony to the importance that was attached to it in the 1950s. Today the attitude that is far more likely to predominate is, 'Does it really matter?' The lack of interest in the status of the intellectual stands in sharp contrast to the passionate debates that surrounded their role in previous times.

We live in a time when books and newspaper articles with titles like *The Last Intellectual* capture a pervasive sense of intellectual disengagement. It is not simply a cultural affectation to describe some very ordinary thinkers as 'the last intellectual'[3] – there do not appear to be very many prominent intellectual voices, and it is difficult to discern their collective impact on society. Indeed, it is the absence of a significant intellectual movement devoted to the advance of a distinct set of ideas to the wider public that illustrates the mood of disengagement.

From a powerful protagonist to a lost soul

The significance of this change in the status of intellectuals can be readily grasped when placed in a historical perspective. Throughout most of the past three centuries, the intellectual

[3] Such as, for example, Ella Taylor's 'The Last Intellectual: Clive James. Renaissance Man', *LA Weekly*: 17 July 2003.

possessed formidable cultural authority and influence. Commentators often had an exaggerated sense of the status of intellectuals, and they were seen to have enormous power to influence events. Intellectuals were frequently portrayed as dangerous subversives who led the assault on the traditional order and who succeeded in unleashing the dark forces of radical destruction. Enlightenment intellectuals were frequently blamed for imposing their ideology of reason on the rest of society. Burke's denunciation of men of letters, who are so 'fond of distinguishing themselves', so 'rarely averse to innovation' and so enamoured 'with their theories about the rights of man that they have totally forgot his nature', provided the prototype for the often-repeated critique of the self-indulgent and disruptive intellectual. Intellectuals were often not liked but they were taken very, very seriously.

Anti-intellectualism represented a strong current of opinion within American culture. Richard Hofstadter's *Anti-Intellectualism in America* provides a graphic account of the influence of this trend. The New England Puritan writer John Cotton warned in 1642 that 'the more learned and witty you bee, the more fit to act for Satan you will be'. Such sentiments of dislike for clever people were motivated by the fear that the intellectual was likely to transgress conventional norms.

Since Burke's time intellectuals have been blamed for virtually every ill that afflicts society. Many a right-wing critic in France blamed Marcel Proust for single-handedly causing the moral decay of the Third Republic. In Britain the Bloomsbury set were represented as the villains in the traditionalist imagination; they were blamed for sowing the seeds of doubt about Britain's imperial mission. They were portrayed as the decadent beneficiaries of Britain's greatness, who took delight in systematically destroying all the values that made up the identity of the nation. In the US, the New York intellectual was often accused of importing un-American ideas into the country. And during the

sixties and seventies, campus radicals were held responsible for
the moral decline of America.

Intellectuals were frequently denounced as treasonous para-
sites or, more charitably, as useful fools. Critics of this treachery
were motivated by the conviction that social disorder and moral
decay were the consequences of the formidable influence of
intellectual demagogues upon the gullible masses. The most
systematic exposition of the theory of the politically motivated
intellectual influencing public opinion to the detriment of society
is to be found in Julien Benda's *The Betrayal of the Intellectual*.
Published in the 1920s, this book denounces intellectuals for
abandoning their role as guardians of the truth for that of
political attachment. He accuses intellectuals of 'divinizing'
politics and of being responsible for the unleashing of political
passions. Benda claims that when intellectuals become involved
in political movements, they give coherence to passions and turn
them into pernicious ideologies. 'Our age is indeed the age of the
intellectual organization of political hatreds', writes Benda.[4] The
linkage of intellectuals with ideologies underpinned numerous
accounts of the explosive mass movements of the twentieth
century.

By the time of the Cold War, the tradition of blaming
intellectuals for political extremism and destruction was well
established. The belief that the intellectual bore a significant
responsibility for the rise of totalitarianism dominates Arthur
Koestler's 1944 article 'The Intelligentsia'. Koestler predicted that
'we are in for an era of managerial super-states' where the
intelligentsia is 'bound to become a special sector in the civil
service'.[5] Joseph Schumpeter saw the intellectual as a threat to the
survival of capitalism. In his major work of the 1940s,
Capitalism, Socialism and Democracy, he argued that the

---

[4] Benda (1959), p. 21.
[5] Koestler (1983), p. 84.

intellectual was responsible for establishing 'the atmosphere of hostility to capitalism'. Similar arguments were repeated in the sixties, when the prevailing sense of disorder and moral malaise was blamed on the actions of the politically motivated radical intellectual.

Denunciations of the destructive legacy of the intellectuals soon claimed that this powerful group had become, or was about to become, a new class. Bertrand de Jouvenel's Cold War polemic against the intellectual argued that it was the intelligentsia that represented the greatest threat to society: 'It has for long been assumed that the great problem of the twentieth century is that of the industrial wage-earner's place in society; insufficient notice has been taken of the rise of a vast intellectual class, whose place in society may prove the greater problem.'[6] Within a decade this argument had acquired the status of a conventional wisdom. Certainly by the 1960s no one would pause to remark that not enough attention had been paid to the role of the intellectual. Interminable discussion about how the intelligentsia had replaced the proletariat as the truly revolutionary class soon followed.

Probably the most influential text dealing with the intellectual in the 1970s and early 1980s was Alvin Gouldner's *The Future of Intellectuals and the Rise of the New Class*. Gouldner claimed that this new class was 'the most progressive force in modern society and in the center of whatever human emancipation is possible in the foreseeable future'.[7] The idea that intellectuals constituted a benign progressive elite was the mirror image of the right-wing denunciation of the new class as a parasitic destructive force. However, both standpoints credited the intellectual with considerable power to influence the course of events.

In retrospect, one is struck by the inflated significance

---

[6]   B. de Jouvenel, 'Treatment of Capitalism by Intellectuals', in Hayek (1954), p. 122.

[7]   Gouldner (1979), p. 83.

attached to the role of the intellectual in the past. Gouldner's caricature of the rise of a new class of intellectuals appears today as an incomprehensible anachronism. So do the passionate denunciations of the Enlightenment Intellectual. Occasionally one encounters a well-rehearsed warning of the intellectual ambition to transform the world. 'One would, however, be ill advised to assume that we have seen the last of the rage to reorder political, social, and economic relations in light of the dictates of theory', cautions one current anti-Enlightenment thinker.[8] But such warnings seem strangely dissonant with today's cultural climate.

Today few look upon the intellectual as a dangerous fanatic threatening the moral fibre of society. To be sure, there is a handful of conservative thinkers on the losing side of the Culture Wars who object to the behaviour of left-wing academics, but their focus is on university politics rather than on the intellectual. Indeed the target is often the mendacious university administrator or bureaucrat rather than the intellectual. Here and there anti-intellectual sentiments still prevail, but they lack a clear focus and do not provoke any serious debate. Insofar as there is any contemporary discussion about the intellectual, it is motivated by concern about what has happened to this figure. In the past, the question 'where are the intellectuals?' could be answered by pointing to a variety of geographical areas – Paris, Berlin, Vienna, St Petersburg, Bloomsbury, Greenwich Village – as sites of intellectual ferment. Today, one would be hard pushed to point to such a place, and campus towns are inhabited by intelligent and well-educated people who work as professional academics rather than as participants in an intellectual milieu.

Intellectuals are rarely represented as having the power to do very much. The most controversial text on the question of the

---

[8]   Paul A. Rahe, 'The Idea of the Public Intellectual in the Age of the Enlightenment', in Melzer, Weinberger and Zinman (eds) (2003), p. 46.

intellectual in recent years is probably Russell Jacoby's *The Last Intellectuals*. This book explores the disappearance of the intellectual from public life and attempts to analyse the causes of the intellectual's diminishing impact upon society. The very fact that today many monographs ask 'what is a public intellectual?' suggests that what they are describing corresponds to an endangered species. With questions posed like 'who are they?' and 'where are they?', it is worth reminding ourselves just what we mean by the concept of an intellectual.

What makes the Intellectual?

Intellectuals are often defined according to their occupations. It is sometimes suggested that people who work with their brains are doing intellectual work – therefore in Western societies, where an ever-decreasing proportion of the population work with their hands, millions of people perform intellectual labour. In addition to obvious candidates like teachers, lawyers and scientists, there is a veritable army of public sector and private sector employees who are employed to perform mental work. However, those involved in non-manual occupations are not necessarily intellectuals. As Ron Eyerman argues, it is important to distinguish between the performance of intellectual labour and intellectuals, because intellectuals' identity 'forms around other kinds of interests than those related to social position'.[9] Intellectuals are not defined according to the jobs they do but the manner in which they act, the way they see themselves, and the values that they uphold.

Being an intellectual is not about how one makes a living. Coser argues that intellectuals 'live for rather than off ideas.' Eyerman echoes this point when he states that 'intellectuals may

[9]   Eyerman (1994), p. 6.

live off their ideas but they must also live for them'.[10] Although the notion of living for an idea may strike the reader as hopelessly idealistic, it has motivated the behaviour of millions of people during recent centuries. Indeed, it can be said that whatever reservation one has about such idealism, it has inspired many to see creative possibilities beyond the sober realities of everyday existence. Even being an academic expert does not lead directly to becoming an intellectual. As the French sociologist Pierre Bourdieu commented, in order to 'claim the title of intellectual', cultural producers 'must deploy their specific expertise and authority in their particular cultural domain in a political activity outside it'.[11] From Bourdieu's standpoint, someone like Einstein exercises intellectual authority when he steps outside his expert field (physics) and comments on the state of global politics. Their sense of identity as an intellectual derives, in part, from participating in a project that transcends any particular occupation or interest. 'The intentional meaning of "being an intellectual" is to rise above the partial preoccupation of one's own profession or artistic *genre* and engage with the global issues of truth, judgement and taste of the time', argues Bauman.[12] Not surprisingly, one of the values most acclaimed by intellectuals is the ability to pursue a life of independence and autonomy. Gouldner believed that autonomy represents a key aspiration for intellectuals, observing that the 'deepest structure in the culture and ideology of intellectuals is their pride in their own *autonomy*'.[13] The desire to possess the freedom to act in accordance with one's belief and reflection strongly motivates the behaviour of the intellectual. That is why intellectuals often exist in a state of creative tension with the rules and restrictions imposed by the prevailing institutions on everyday life.

[10]   Coser (1965), p. viii and Eyerman (1994), p. 13.
[11]   Bourdieu (1989), p. 99.
[12]   Bauman (1987), p. 2.
[13]   Gouldner (1979), p. 33.

To feel and behave like an intellectual requires at least a mental distancing from the conventions and pressures of everyday affairs. Eyerman noted that 'the more intellectual labour is controlled by external forces, rules and procedures, supervisors and so on, the less of an intellectual one feels oneself to be'.[14] The aspiration for autonomy is driven by the understanding that ideas cannot be developed in accordance with a schedule or the dictates of a particular institution. It is generally recognized that a degree of detachment is essential for the gaining of perspective and of creativity. Intellectuals can be employed by institutions, but if their imagination and work remains confined to these institutions they will become simply experts and technocrats. An important American study published in the 1960s argued that if intellectuals were absorbed into the 'establishment', this 'would spell the end of intellectuals as recent history has known them'. The author warned that such a development would not serve the interests of America, since 'only if intellectuals preserve critical intelligence, maintain some remoteness from day-to-day tasks, and cultivate concern with ultimate rather than with proximate values can they serve society fully'.[15]

Even in the most favourable periods for cultural development, intellectuals tend to have an uneasy relationship with the status quo. There are, of course, mandarin intellectuals who serve the dominant oligarchy. But such mandarins quickly turn into ideologues and apologists and become alienated from intellectual pursuits. They swiftly compromise their authority as intellectuals. It is difficult to envisage how intellectual work can be advanced in a way that is entirely conformist. Both conservative and radical intellectuals interpret the world through the prism of principles that are in a state of permanent tension with the practical affairs of society. One group criticizes the prevailing state of affairs in

[14] Eyerman (1994), p. 12.
[15] Cited in Coser (1965), pp. 358–9.

order to move society backward, and the other to transform certain aspects of it.

The creative role of an intellectual requires detachment from any particular identity and interest. Since the beginning of modernity, the authority of the intellectual has rested on the claim to be acting and speaking on behalf of society as a whole. The intellectual can be seen as the personification of the Enlightenment legacy and has traditionally sought to represent the standpoint of universality. Through their embrace of universalism, modern intellectuals 'have constituted themselves as they are in and by their rejection of particularism', observes Pierre Bourdieu.[16] Through speaking for values that transcend specific experience – reason, rationality, science, freedom – intellectuals reaffirm the salience of the Enlightenment project.

Regardless of individual temperament, intellectuals are often forced to challenge contemporary wisdom and convention. The potential for such conflict is contained within the universalist perspective, which contradicts the customs and conventions pragmatically constructed to guide the life of particular groups. As Edward Said noted, acting on the principles of universalism is a risky business. 'Universality means taking a risk in order to go beyond the easy certainties provided us by our background, language, nationality, which so often shields us from the reality of others.'[17] It is because intellectuals of a universalist persuasion often raise disturbing questions about prevailing customs and assumptions that they are often perceived as unpatriotic cosmopolitan outsiders. Orwell's criticism of intellectuals who are 'ashamed of their nationality' is paradigmatic in this respect.[18] The detached individual, who does not quite conform to the prevailing norms, was a part of the stereotype of the twentieth-century intellectual.

---

[16] Bourdieu (1989), p. 110.
[17] Said (1994), p. xii
[18] See Orwell 1941), pp. 46–8.

Not all intellectuals subscribe to the philosophical and political outlook of the Enlightenment. Over the years, conservative intellectuals have been animated by their distaste for Enlightenment values. But in the very act of seeking to uphold their version of tradition against the claims of the Enlightenment, they too have had to go beyond their particular experience and adopt a more cosmopolitan outlook. Their critique is as much a product of the Enlightenment as the Enlightenment is the object of their rancour. Conservative intellectuals are no less the product of the Enlightenment than their more radical counterparts.

Being an intellectual implies social engagement. It is difficult to live for ideas and not attempt to influence society. It involves not only being involved in creative mental activity, but also the assumption of social responsibility and taking a political stand. Not every intellectual has a disposition for social engagement but, as a group, intellectuals are drawn towards political life. Regis Debray in his study of French intellectuals states that it is not the level of education that defines the intellectual but the 'project of influencing the public'. Debray characterizes this orientation as a moral project that is essentially political.[19] Such a project is not necessarily a party political one, but one that is prepared to conduct a battle for the public hearts and minds.

There are numerous definitions of the intellectual. They are sometimes depicted as the defenders of cultural standards, as a group of perpetual critics and dissenters, as the conscience of society. Lewis Coser defines intellectuals as 'men who never seem satisfied with things as they are'. But he understands that the most fruitful way of understanding intellectuals is in relation to the realm of ideas.[20] Many observers believe that one of the distinguishing features of the intellectual is his or her ability to engage with the wider issues of the day. 'The intentional meaning

[19] Debray (1981), p. 127.
[20] Coser (1965), p. viii.

of "being an intellectual" is to rise above the partial preoccupation of one's own profession or artistic *genre* and engage with the
global issues of truth, judgement and taste of the time', argues
Bauman.[21] According to Edward Said, intellectuals assume their
role through representing the standpoint of a constituency or of a
wider public: 'My argument is that intellectuals are individuals
with a vocation for the art of representing, whether that is
talking, writing, teaching, appearing on television.'[22] One of the
simplest, yet most useful, definitions of the intellectual is
provided by Seymour Lipset. According to Lipset, intellectuals
are 'all those who create, distribute, and apply *culture*, that is, the
symbolic order of man, including art, science, and religion'.[23]
Whatever definition we prefer, being an intellectual involves an
intimate relationship to the pursuit of ideas and of truth.

Of course intellectuals do not all share the same philosophy
and political outlook. They live for different ideas. But despite
differences, which are sometimes bitter and far-reaching,
intellectuals share a common desire to influence the world. In
particular they possess a common commitment to being the
critical voice of the truth as they see it. The powerful American
social commentator C. Wright Mills argued that 'in the first
instance the politics of the intellectual are "the politics of truth" '.
He took the view that through the pursuit of the truth, the
intellectual held the powers-that-be to account. 'Whatever else
the intellectual may be, surely he is among those who ask serious
questions, and, if he is a political intellectual, he asks his
questions of those with power.'[24]

There is little doubt that the portrait of the intellectual
depicted above provides an idealized version of the workings of

---

21 Bauman (1987), p. 2.
22 Said (1994), p. 10.
23 Lipset (1960), p. 311.
24 C. Wright Mills, 'On Knowledge and Power', pp. 611–12 in Horowitz
    (1963).

this group. Throughout the past three centuries most intellectuals were not full-time crusaders for truth. Like anyone else, intellectuals often compromise, withdraw under pressure and conform to the cultural climate that prevails. Sometimes they can trade in their autonomy for an easy life and sometimes their idealism is merely a mask for the ruthless pursuit of self-interest. But whatever the trajectory and characteristics of individual intellectuals, as a group they have played an important role in questioning conventions and sensitizing society to ideals and values that have helped to push forward human progress.

Today, the role of critical engagement with ideas is often associated with what is sometimes described as the 'traditional intellectual'. The very fact that the word traditional is used in qualification indicates that existence of this type of person is now directly put to question. Just as Truth is often represented as lacking authority, so too people who claim to pursue it are dismissed as an anachronistic irrelevance. That is why the relevance of the role of the 'traditional critical intellectual' to today's conditions is frequently interrogated. Even commentators who are sympathetic to the exercise of intellectual authority believe that its 'traditional role has eroded'. 'Perhaps we have to re-evaluate the meaning and the importance of the category of the traditional intellectual itself as well as analyze its changing conditions' states Katrin Fridjonsdottir, a perceptive commentator on this subject.[25] So what are the influences that have made contemporary society relatively inhospitable to the survival of the so-called traditional intellectual?

---

[25] Katrin Fridjonsdottir (1987), 'The Modern Intellectual: In Power or Disarmed? Reflections on the Sociology of Intellectuals and Intellectual Work', in Eyerman, Svensson and Soderquist (1987), p. 113.

Contemporary society and the intellectual

Some of the structural changes associated with the decline of the traditional intellectual have been the growing impact of the market upon intellectual life, the institutionalization and the professionalization of intellectual life, the growing power of the media and the erosion of public space for the exercise of autonomy. Many writers on this subject claim that the main driving force behind the transformation of the intellectual landscape has been the relentless expansion of academia. According to this perspective, academic careerism has dealt a serious body blow to the continued vitality of intellectual life.[26]

The rise of the expert and of the professional has been a significant feature of capitalist societies for some time. Since the 1950s, this trend has become highly visible and now exercises a powerful influence on how authority is perceived. Those who portray intellectuals as a 'new class' often argue that professionalism serves as an ideology that now underpins the authority of the ruling elites. From this perspective, it is possible to draw the conclusion that intellectuals are more powerful than in previous times. This approach was systematically advanced in the 1970s by Gouldner, who claimed that 'professionalism silently installs the New Class as the paradigm of virtuous and legitimate authority, performing with technical skill and dedicated concern for society-at-large'.[27]

It is doubtful that the ascendancy of professional authority has boosted the influence of the intellectual. The mental work of the professional is focused on the provision of services, not the promotion of ideas. Insofar as ideas are involved in the delivery of a professional task, they are not valued for their own sake but as a means to their realization. It is not the performance of

---

[26] This point is well argued by Jacoby (1987).
[27] Gouldner (1979), p. 19.

intellectual labour or any specific economic function that defines intellectuals. Intellectuals are constituted through their relationship to society and the development of ideas. And whatever their occupations, it is not directly through their jobs that they exercise their role as intellectuals.

Contrary to the new class thesis, the expansion of professionalism may well create new obstacles to the pursuit of intellectual activity. Professionalism promotes values and forms of behaviour that may well be inconsistent with those of the intellectual. Activities such as offering a critique of the status quo, acting as the conscience of society, or pursuing the truth regardless of the consequences are not what the job of a professional is all about. As Katrin Fridjonsdottir remarks, a professional expert might be a critical intellectual but 'he is definitely not expected to behave like one in his role as an expert'.[28] Indeed the forms of behaviour associated with the professional expert are very different to the way that intellectuals act. That is why many writers on the subject believe that professionalism constitutes the most significant threat facing the intellectual. The inconsistency between the ethos of professionalism and that of the intellectual was spelled out by Edward Said:

> By professionalism I mean thinking of your work as an intellectual as something you do for a living, between the hours of nine and five with one eye on the clock, and another cocked at what is considered to be proper, professional behaviour – not rocking the boat, not straying outside the accepted paradigms or limits, making yourself marketable and above all presentable, hence uncontroversial and unpolitical and 'objective'.[29]

[28] Katrin Fridjonsdottir (1987), 'The Modern Intellectual: In Power or Disarmed? Reflections on the Sociology of Intellectuals and Intellectual Work', in Eyerman (1987), p. 121.

[29] Said (1994), p. 55.

Once intellectual work becomes professionalized, it ceases to possess its independence and potential for asking difficult questions of society. Instead it acquires a managerial or technocratic function.

Paradoxically, it appears that the very growth in the demand for intellectual labour has thrown up new obstacles to the exercise of intellectual activity. The flourishing of a market for ideas has encouraged the professionalization of intellectual work. And as Eyerman noted, through moving intellectual labour from the margin to the centre of society the market has acquired an unprecedented influence over the conduct of intellectual life. The result of this process has been the institutionalization of many of the functions associated with the activity of the intellectual:

> Those institutions and processes which traditionally have been formative for intellectuals – the university, the literary and political public sphere, especially as connected to cultural and class conflict – have in late modern societies become more and more institutionalized, professionalized and commercialized. The role of the social critic, so central to one traditional ideal of the intellectual, has itself been institutionalized to such an extent that the 'intellectual' has become a permanent feature on television talk shows and on the 'culture' pages of the more serious newspapers.[30]

So although intellectual work is more in evidence than in previous times, these are functions performed by institutions and their professionals rather than by intellectuals. Those intellectuals who attempt to transmit their ideas through the media often turn into talking heads servicing the show. They often find that they are tolerated only insofar as they provide sound bites and entertainment.

The institutionalization of intellectual work has a significant

---

[30] Eyerman (1994), p. 191.

impact on the way that ideas interact with society. As professionals and experts, even as academic experts, intellectuals' authority rests not on the quality of their ideas, but on the claim to expertise. The language they speak becomes increasingly technical and specialized, and not a vernacular that can be understood by the public. The new language of the academic expert reflects a lifestyle that is devoted to a narrow specialism. Through this process, the very content of intellectual activity alters. Fridjonsdottir has drawn attention to the way that activities such as literary criticism have become almost '[an] exclusively professionalized activity of predominantly academically trained persons'. She claims that this has changed both the form and the content of this activity, so that a literary critic who fails to keep up with new fashions in cultural criticism is not likely to survive long in his or her profession.[31]

The manifest tendency towards the professionalization of intellectual life has led some writers on this subject to question the viability of the role of the independent intellectual. It is frequently suggested that the pressure of the market also directly impacts on the realm of ideas. A high level of specialization encourages knowledge to become more and more fragmented, which undermines the ability of the intellectual to engage with society as a whole. Writing in this vein, Eyerman points to the 'power of market forces to determine the content of cultural production'.[32]

There is little doubt that the power of market forces can have a significant influence over the content of cultural production. But it is not the market that has led to the retreat of the intellectual. In previous times, intellectuals thrived through reacting against the market – today, they are more likely to attempt to realize their

---

[31] Katrin Fridjonsdottir (1987), 'The Modern Intellectual: In Power or Disarmed? Reflections on the Sociology of Intellectuals and Intellectual Work', in Eyerman (1987), p. 121.

[32] Eyerman (1994), p. 92.

ambition through it. The idea that intellectuals have been the unwitting victims of circumstances beyond their control overlooks the fact that they have tended to embrace the opportunities offered through the institutionalization of intellectual work. Intellectuals have played a key role in promoting specialisms and academic disciplines. The idealism of the intellectual has given way to pragmatism, and a distinctly instrumentalist approach towards life.

The sense of intellectual independence has given way to a demand for institutional affirmation and recognition. This development is particularly striking in the contemporary debates that surround the absence of the public intellectual. The debate that began as an attempt to account for the decline of the independent intellectual has turned into a demand by some of its contributors that institutions and public bodies help rescue the public intellectual from extinction. Some American universities have responded to this concern as if it were a market opportunity, and have launched graduate programmes designed to train public intellectuals. Others have called upon public institutions to do more to promote the activity of the intellectual. Writing in this vein, two American academics state:

> Finally, we call for greater institutional and material recognition of these multiple forms of public intellectual work. This includes both valuing and fostering public work. For example, for those who pursue service learning, institutions might provide or require training or certification, involve all faculty in some sort of service learning, and provide release time or course load reduction for those who elaborately embed themselves in community work.[33]

The demand for certifying public intellectual work indicates just how much the idea of intellectual independence has given way to

[33] Brouwer and Squires (2003), p. 212.

the ethos of professionalization. When intellectual identity is made contingent upon institutional approval, then it clearly ceases to have anything in common with the classical aspiration for intellectual autonomy.

It is difficult to explain the credentialist mentality of today's professional thinker as the direct consequence of the power of market forces. No doubt the expansion of the market for professionals and experts has influenced developments, but it cannot account for the readiness with which people have adopted forms of behaviour that are inconsistent with the role of the traditional intellectual. To understand why this occurred, it is necessary to look for explanations beyond the structural changes that affect the conduct of intellectual work.

The devaluation of the role of the intellectual

Although changes to the structure of society have important implications for understanding the demise of the intellectual, they do not explain why its status has become devalued. In particular, at a time when education, knowledge and intellectual labour are in such high demand, why should there be so many question marks raised over the survival of the traditional critical intellectual? Whatever the answer to this question, it is evident that most contributions on this subject have given up on the traditional critical intellectual, and are busy attempting to find a new role for the intellectual.

It is widely believed that in the so-called postmodern era, where the fundamental tenets of the Enlightenment have been called into question, the role of the critical intellectual has been severely compromised. Since many of the ideals associated with the exercise of intellectual authority – the search for knowledge, the application of reason – have become targets of scepticism, the work of the intellectual has lost some of its cultural appeal. The decline of belief in the power of reasoning has significantly weakened the status of the intellectual. An all-embracing view of the world, which was said to influence the outlook of the classical intellectual, has given way to the conviction that such a broad outlook is beyond the capacity of the human imagination.

As a result, the intellectual has been assigned a role that is far more limited than was the case in the past. Even those who retain a positive point of reference towards the critical intellectual appear to believe that it can only survive in a seriously modified form. 'While the contexts for their emergence may have been narrowed, and the range of possibilities thereby reduced, the traditions that constitute the intellectual are more than just a fading memory,' writes Eyerman. But despite the attempt to reassure that the traditions associated with the intellectual are 'more than just a fading memory', Eyerman ends up with a fairly modest and pessimistic vision of the future of intellectual work. 'Although its meaning has been almost entirely altered by what has been called the postmodern condition, the concept of the intellectual still provides a living resource which is likely to be called upon as a rallying cry for coming generations of dissidents.'[34]

The belief that the 'postmodern condition' has fundamentally transformed the terrain of intellectual activity has had a powerful impact on the way thinkers think about themselves and their activities. Unlike the Enlightenment intellectual who acclaimed the vision of universalism, today's thinkers are much more likely to celebrate a particularistic identity. Today we have English intellectuals, Black intellectuals, Feminist, Gay and Jewish intellectuals. As a result, intellectual authority does not rest on the ability to represent the truth but on the capacity to affirm the identity of a particular group or specialism. The shift from a universalist to a particularistic focus should not be seen as merely

---

[34] Eyerman (1994), pp. 199 and 200.

a variation in scale. It involves a fundamental redefinition of intellectual ambition from the attempt to go beyond particular experience to the desire to affirm it.[35] Such affirmation is dominated by an intensely conservative imperative that is hostile to the critical questioning of society.

Bauman argues that one of the consequences of post-modernity is a fundamental change in the role of the intellectual from that of a legislator to that of an interpreter. In their legislator role, intellectuals make authoritative statements that have a direct bearing on the shaping of public opinion. In their role as postmodern interpreter, intellectuals are in the business of facilitating communication – translating statements made within one communally based tradition, so that they can be understood within the system of knowledge based on another tradition.[36]

The downsizing of intellectual authority was vigorously advocated by Michel Foucault, who took the view that since there is no truly universal truth, intellectuals cannot be in the business of conveying universal truth. He claimed that thinkers could aspire to be, not universal, but 'specific' intellectuals. Specific intellectuals are not expected to make broad pronouncements about the problems of the world – rather they are able to devote their work to areas in which they have the most expertise, thus acquiring tangible results.

Views such as those held by Bauman and Foucault reflect the experience of demoralization with the workings of the Enlightenment legacy. But whereas Bauman recognizes the importance for intellectuals to promote the 'process of enlightenment', Foucault is delighted with the demise of the universalist intellectual. For Foucault and others who are attracted to the outlook of postmodernism, the present era of intellectual life

---

[35] These points are developed in Furedi (1992), chapter 8.
[36] Bauman (1987), pp. 4–5.

actually represents a major advance over the past.[37] The reigning
in of intellectual energy is often depicted as a responsible and
pragmatic accommodation to the demands of postmodern times,
and there is a palpable sense of satisfaction with compromise
among the new breed of postmodernist conformist intellectuals.

The conformist intellectual

Intellectuals in the past were often concerned about attempts to
undermine the pursuit of their activities. Political intervention
directed at intellectual autonomy and the commercial pressures of
the market were often criticized by the radical intelligentsia.
Today, radical voices are less inclined to be concerned about
attacks on free speech, censorship and the battle for ideas.
Whereas criticism of the traditional critical intellectual was
previously voiced mainly by the polemicists of the political right,
today it is far more likely to be articulated by the left. So the
introduction to a recently published collection of essays on the
subject of the intellectual by a leftist academic, patronizingly
dismisses the 'older and less morally creditable conception of
intellectuals'.[38]

In previous times, radical intellectuals often confronted the
upholders of tradition to demand change and the transformation
of cultural life. That is why the most strident anti-intellectual
voices tended to be the upholders of tradition. Today, it is no
longer the representatives of cultural conservatism who celebrate
and seek to defend the status quo. On the contrary, intellectuals

---

[37] Since postmodernists tend to eschew definitions, postmodern is a fluid and
confusing concept that is difficult to define. Postmodernists are hostile to
the idea that truth can be objective, are sceptical of the authority of science
and resist the idea of progress.

[38] See Bruce Robbins, 'Introduction: The grounding of Intellectuals', in
Robbins (1990), p. xiv.

of the right are often appalled by cultural life and would like to see fundamental institutional and cultural changes. The defence of cultural and educational institutions, which is traditionally assumed by the political right, has been adopted by professionals and experts involved in intellectual work.

A profound mood of new conservatism shapes deliberations on the role of the intellectual. There has never been a period since the beginning of modernity when people working with ideas were so complacent about their role. This atmosphere of conformism is particularly evident among professional academics. Any suggestion that intellectual life faces exhaustion, or is in any sense inferior to what existed in previous times, is perfunctorily dismissed as a despicable attempt to return to some elitist inspired mythical age. According to one such account, 'for intellectuals, there is certainly no need to despair', since 'the life that goes on in the university, the pedagogy we conduct amid the ruins, is different from, livelier and more rigorous than, what the various legends of the truth's decline and the intellectual's demise have led us to believe'. The author of these words even has a few crumbs of comfort to offer to those concerned with the marginalization of the Enlightenment tradition. 'For those who get it, the values of the Enlightenment still furnish the patches of brightness by which we choose our way,' he writes.[39] Finding 'patches of brightness' in order to avoid engaging with the retreat of the intellectual seems to be the dominant response to the problem.

Following Foucault, many contributors are positively delighted that the Enlightenment stands are now discredited. Andrew Ross is pleased that the agenda is no longer dominated by a universalist outlook. For Ross, 'the withering away of the universal intellectual' represents a positive step forward. He reserves his scorn for those who still yearn for the intellectual culture of a previous era, and denounces what he calls the

[39] Michael (2000), pp. 174–5.

'reactionary consensus of left and right, each unswervingly loyal to their respective narratives of decline'. Ross dismisses charges of 'post-sixties fragmentation and academification from unreconstructed voices on the left, and warnings of doom and moral degeneracy from the Cassandras on the right'.[40] In this view, all is well – the only flies in the ointment are the twisted critics of the professionalization of academic life.

The assumption that classical intellectual authority is no longer sustainable informs today's conformist cultural outlook. 'For those who take seriously the diagnosis that public life in Western democracies is no longer of a kind that permits claims to general intellectual authority, declinism, of whatever political coloring, is too plainly a posture rather than an answer', argues the editor of a collection of articles on 'The Public Intellectual'.[41] Serious concern with the malaise of intellectual life often invites the smug response that all is well in academia. The questioning of contemporary intellectual and pedagogic practices is frequently dismissed as a lament for a golden age. This complacent defence of the status quo is virtually unprecedented in the intellectual history of modernity. In the nineteenth century, even the most conservative section of the intelligentsia was critical of the prevailing cultural climate, and every brand of intellectuals sought to alter, improve, transform and even overthrow the world that confronted them. The contrast between this tradition of intellectual ferment, and the complacent attitudes displayed today, highlights the distinct features of intellectual life in the early twenty-first century.

One of the most systematic endorsements of intellectual conformism is presented in the writings of Bruce Robbins, professor of English at Rutgers University. Robbins appears as a wholehearted supporter of academic professionalism because he believes that it has created an environment hospitable to new

---

[40] Ross (1989), pp. 211 and 229.
[41] Small (2002), p. 5.

minority voices.[42] Robbins embraces academic professionalism on account of the fact that that the cultural left has thrived and benefited in this environment. 'Thanks to the Reaganite backlash, much of the public has thus learned that, for better or worse, the left has a powerful presence in American cultural life,' he brags. Robbins also boasts of the left's own 'cultural and institutional achievements' and writes of the 'grounding of intellectuals' in universities.[43] Robbins does not merely applaud the success of the left in 'grounding itself within American educational and cultural institutions since the 1960s' – he self-consciously deprecates the legacy of the 'old' intellectuals and their 'abysmal record' of behaviour.[44]

Although Robbins continually alludes to the supposed triumph of the cultural left, what he is really describing is the displacement of the vocation of the intellectual by the academic professional. His lack of concern with the erosion of the independence and autonomy of the intellectual is matched by a pragmatic adaptation to the demands of academic institutionalism. From this standpoint, the devaluation of the role of intellectual autonomy is represented as a positive blow against old-fashioned elitism. The new intellectual gains authority from his institution, and does not require a sense of autonomy. Of course not every academic acquiesces to the institutionalization of intellectual life and adopts the conformist identity of a housekept thinker. And many institutionalized intellectuals yearn to achieve a degree of autonomy from institutional pressures. Most academics tend to be intelligent professionals and astute experts, who sadly are not culturally equipped to play the role of the public intellectual. They belong to their institutions and remain estranged from the world of the public.

---

[42] Robbins (1993), chapter 1.
[43] See Bruce Robbins, 'Introduction: The Grounding of Intellectuals', in Robbins (1990), pp. x and xi.
[44] See Bruce Robbins, 'Introduction: The Grounding of Intellectuals' in Robbins (1990), p. xiii.

2   Trivial Pursuits

Contemporary Western society has a love–hate relationship with knowledge. On one hand we pursue it and celebrate it, employing people to gain knowledge of market conditions, the mood of the nation or what makes your three-year-old child tick. Since September 11, opinion-makers have often complained that we simply do not know enough about why terrorism has become such a global threat or why Muslim societies appear to resent the West. It seems that we don't have enough people with a colloquial knowledge of Middle East languages. To put it crudely, we are worried about our lack of knowledge and fear that we may be deficient in intelligence about what is going on in large chunks of the world. We take Knowledge very, very seriously, as expressions like 'knowledge is power' only confirm.

At the same time, however, society is uncomfortable with the pursuit of knowledge, and often distrustful of those who claim to know. There is widespread suspicion of scientific authority, and people who attempt to extend the boundaries of scientific knowledge find themselves accused of 'playing God'. Such accusations are not only levelled at individuals involved in controversial areas like genetic research or nanotechnology, but also at those who attempt to gain a better understanding of human health in general. Social scientists who seek knowledge with a capital K are disparaged for their attachment to 'meta-narratives' with the same intensity that is generally directed at genetic research. In the past, it was often said that a 'little knowledge is a dangerous thing'. Today, society is confronted with a strong undercurrent of opinion that suggests that 'too much knowledge threatens human survival'.

The co-existence of an insatiable appetite for more knowledge and an intense suspicion of its further development is one of the paradoxes of Western culture today. The constant demand for scientific evidence exists alongside apprehensions about what the scientist is up to in the laboratory. The massive investment in education, universities and private research has not led to the flourishing of a public scientific, cultural or intellectual discourse. The younger generations appear to be turned off by mathematics and science, and it is not intellectual curiosity but hostility and suspicion that animates the debates on these subjects. Nor has public reaction against experimentation and progress led to the establishment of alternative outlets for the development of intellectual curiosity. In previous times, when young people became estranged from science they turned to the humanities and liberal arts. Today's generation of students has adopted a distinctly pragmatic approach, and is as turned off by history, social theory and philosophy as it is by science. In the US, between 1970 and 1995, the number of history majors graduated by American colleges and universities decreased by 39 per cent, foreign language majors declined by 37 per cent, and English departments lost 10 per cent of their students.[1] And this decline occurred at a time when the numbers attending colleges has increased at a steady rate! The public's unease towards existing scientific knowledge is complemented by a tangible sense of indifference towards its further development.

The public's unease with the development of knowledge does not, however, mean that it has ceased to be curious about how the world works. There is an enormous public appetite for popular science books. Historical biographies often make the

---

[1]   Russell Berman and Stephen Haber, 'Whatever Happened to the Academic Left?', *Hoover Digest*, 2002, no. 2.

bestseller lists, while television programmes devoted to historical and scientific themes can always secure a substantial audience of curious individuals. Many people really want to learn about the world. But in a world where the pursuit of knowledge lacks powerful cultural affirmation, people's relation to it acquires a passive character. Yes, people buy popular science books but they rarely get together to discuss and debate the issues they contain. Many individuals have sought to exploit the opportunities provided by the Internet to pursue their ideas or to learn about subjects that interest them. But this welcome development is driven as much by suspicion of official sources of knowledge as it is by the impulse for exploring new ideas.

Society's uneasy relationship to knowledge is influenced by the same forces that are responsible for the changing status of the intellectual. The authoritative status that modernity has traditionally assigned to knowledge has come under challenge from a variety of sources: disappointment with the promise of the Enlightenment and Modernity; a sense of powerlessness regarding our ability to know the future; the consequent growth in the influence of a relativist approach towards knowledge; and the replacement of the pursuit of Knowledge with a pragmatic focus on specialist micro-knowledges.

Disenchantment with the Enlightenment tradition

From its conception, the Enlightenment was subject to hostility and criticism. Opponents of the Enlightenment were bitterly suspicious of the claim that the human capacity to reason could ensure steady progress and improve the condition of life. From the outset, advocates of the Enlightenment were accused of playing God. The optimistic humanist celebration of the capacity to know was dismissed by religious and conservative philosophers as a malevolent project designed to undermine the realm of the sacred. Opponents of the Enlightenment believed that rationality undermined the spiritual connections that linked people to God, to their traditions and communities. It was felt that any strategy to achieve rational change must upset the existing precarious balance and inevitably make things worse.

Rationalism was also decried, because it was felt to be antithetical to the flourishing of the human soul. Anti-Enlightenment critics claimed that the privileged status assigned to reason marginalized the spiritual and moral dimension of life. The promotion of reason and scientific knowledge was held responsible for the decline of religion and consequently the creation of a spiritual or emotional vacuum. It was even suggested that the loss of previously held spiritual certainties was responsible for the growth of fanaticism and totalitarianism. According to Conor Cruise O'Brien, the Enlightenment created an 'emotional vacuum' which was filled by nationalism. The bitter Europe-wide war that ensued is therefore represented as an indirect legacy of the Enlightenment, and before even a plea for mitigation can be entered, he insists that 'the responsibility, though indirect, was real, through the creation of that cosmic emotional vacuum'.[2]

Anxiety towards the pursuit of knowledge and reason was motivated by the conviction that it would disrupt the precarious balance that existed between different groups in society. Anti-Enlightenment thinkers genuinely believed that knowledge was dangerous because it threatened to weaken the faith and beliefs that helped keep the otherwise irrational masses from disrupting society. It was felt that too much education and knowledge would contribute to an explosion of instability, since what held the masses in check was religion and deference to authority. That is

---

[2]   C. Cruise O'Brien, 'Paradise Lost', in *New York Review of Books*, 25 April 1991, p. 58.

why many upholders of tradition feared the advance of reason. As the conservative philosopher Joseph de Maistre explained:

> Man's cradle must be surrounded by dogmas and when his reason awakens, he must find all his opinions already made, at least those concerning his social behaviour. Nothing is more important for man than prejudice.[3]

In this anti-modernist imagination, prejudice and dogma were directly linked to the enforcement of order and the maintenance of cohesion. By contrast, knowledge and reason were greeted as the harbingers of uncertainty, confusion and instability.

It is important to recall that the anti-Enlightenment reaction of the nineteenth century remained subordinate to the prevailing sense of dynamism and progress. Overall, public enthusiasm for science, and a general belief in the power of reason and progress, encouraged a positive cultural valuation of knowledge. In such circumstances experimentation, change and even revolution were often interpreted as symptoms of historical progress. As William Wordsworth wrote in celebration of the French Revolution:

> Bliss was it in that dawn to be alive
> To be young was very heaven

Today Wordsworth's sentiments appear incongruent with social attitudes towards change. The fear of change filters into every aspect of social thought. The pervasive existence of this sentiment has been underwritten by the overwhelming image of failure associated with past attempts at social transformation. The conclusion drawn by most commentaries is that the attempt to change society leads to a situation that is actually worse than what existed previously. It is claimed that the attempt to pursue public policies wedded to rationalism have in fact made the situation far worse. Knowledge, ideas and especially ideologies

---

[3]   Cited in Giner (1976), p. 40.

linked to the Enlightenment, are denounced on the grounds that they bear responsibility for much of the destruction inflicted on people in the twentieth century. One British political columnist has argued that 'transformational ideologies have inflicted vast harm upon our century and a death toll numbering many millions'.[4] This observation resonates with the widely held disenchantment with the legacy of the Enlightenment.

The tendency to limit the application of reason has become a dominant feature of Western intellectual life. In a recent survey of this subject, the well-known American sociologist Jeffrey Alexander wrote about the 'omnipresence of irrationality'. According to Alexander, reason 'has been experienced as a hollow shell, progress as inconceivable, and often actually undesirable'.[5] Even proponents of the Enlightenment find it difficult to promote a robust view of the world that is embedded in the values of reason and progress. The best-case scenario that Morris Berman's *The Twilight of American Culture* is able to posit is one where 'we do have renaissance, a preservation and transmission of Enlightenment culture but only for a select few, and their impact on the rest of culture is apparently nonexistent'.[6] The reaction against reason today is far stronger than at any time since the development of capitalism. In the nineteenth century, the romantic revolt against reason did not question the possibility of knowing: it merely challenged one possible – that is, the rational – form of knowing. Today, the very possibility of knowing has been called into question by people who claim that the world has become far too complex to understand.

The reaction against the Enlightenment can also be understood as a rejection of the authority of knowledge. The argument that human knowledge is limited is consistently used

---

[4] Peter Jenkins, 'New Dreams of Liberty', in *Independent*, 14 May 1991.
[5] Alexander, 'Between progress ...', in Alexander and Sztompka (1990), p. 26.
[6] Berman (2001).

to discredit attempts to improve social circumstances through public policy or scientific advance. The depreciation of reason and understanding justifies the politics of scepticism towards intellectual authority, science and Knowledge. In previous decades, this attitude was most vigorously promoted by individuals on the right wing of the political spectrum. Irrationalist thinkers of the nineteenth century, such as Nietzsche and Schopenhauer, argued that it is ignorance rather than knowledge that characterizes the human condition. Theirs was a history where chaos and chance are far more significant than meaning. Unease with the potential for reasoning was also evident among many of the founders and leading lights of the new social sciences. Max Weber, who remains to this day one of the most influential sociologists, believed that there were important limits to the application of reason. He took the view that reason had little relevance for understanding values. In contrast to the permanence of art, Weber regarded science as having only a transient existence. 'In science, each of us knows that what he has accomplished will be antiquated in ten, twenty, fifty years', he wrote.[7] The restricted role that Weber assigned to reasoning was motivated by his doubts about the possibility of knowing. Today, the dominant critique of rationality is more likely to be influenced by the *fear* of knowledge. There is an influential body of thought that claims that Enlightenment rationality has been responsible for some of the most destructive episodes of human history, while the experience of modernity is often dismissed as a destructive one that logically culminated in the Holocaust. According to one account, the attempt to exterminate Jewish people was an 'exercise in the rational management of society'.[8] This thesis posits the 'promotion of rationality' as a heartless amoral cause that is indifferent to the

[7]   Cited in Furedi (1992), p. 206.
[8]   Bauman (1991), p. 72.

sanctity of life, and therefore possesses a capacity for 'generating the Holocaust-like solution'.[9]

Today, the most bitter denunciations of the Enlightenment come, not from the right, but from radical voices who believe that the very pursuit of knowledge through science, technology and innovation threatens the world. They point to tragic events like the Holocaust as proof of the threat represented by the single-minded pursuit of rationality and knowledge. The far more plausible idea that associates the Holocaust with the triumph of irrationality and the failure to develop the potential of the Enlightenment tradition is sadly overlooked. Instead, the potential for unleashing the power of destruction overwhelms the contemporary imagination. It is the destructive, not the creative, potential of knowledge that shapes today's public imagination.

A sense of powerlessness in the face of uncertainty

Disappointment with the promise of the Enlightenment has diminished public confidence in society's ability to know, understand and ultimately control the future. The view that we live in a world that is so complex as to render meaningless the claim to know is systematically promoted by radical critics of modernity. Critics are also worried that the advance of knowledge itself creates problems, because it threatens to encourage activity and behaviour whose consequences cannot be known in advance. This attitude is most forcefully expressed in the view that one of the products of science and knowledge is risk.

Leading sociologists Ulrich Beck and Anthony Giddens forcefully argue the case for the close association between the sense of risk and the increase of knowledge. 'Many of the

[9] Bauman (1991), pp. 28 and 29.

uncertainties which face us today have been created by the very growth of knowledge', wrote Giddens, and Beck has noted that the 'sources of danger are no longer ignorance but knowledge'.[10] In this scenario, knowledge through its application creates both new hazards and an awareness of their risk. The claim that the problem is not ignorance but knowledge fundamentally questions the authority of science. The implicit preference of ignorance over knowledge represents a contemporary variant of the conservative embrace of prejudice in the nineteenth century. In both cases, knowledge is perceived as undesirable because of its disruptive and disorienting effect.

The association of knowledge with risk is based on a model of society that is uncomfortable with change and uncertainty, and feels continually under threat from technological development. Such a society experiences the advance of knowledge and the unintended consequences of technological development as a source of anxiety and disorientation. These days, arguments that associate knowledge with risks are implicitly questioning the human potential for knowing. It is claimed that human knowledge cannot grasp the chaotic patterns of events set in motion by global capitalism, and the impossibility of knowing or calculating the consequences of technology and human action is widely insisted upon. This view is justified by the argument that technological development in a globalized environment has become so complex as to destroy the foundation for understanding the future. As a result, the German sociologist Nikolas Luhmann claims that 'no one is in a position to claim knowledge of the future nor the capacity to change it'.[11] For Luhmann, knowledge is restricted to providing insights about what has already happened, and rather limited insights at that.

---

[10]   A. Giddens, 'Risk, Trust, Reflexivity', in Beck *et al.* (1994), p. 85 and Beck (1992), p. 183.

[11]   Luhman (1993), p. 48.

Frequently, risk is conceptualized in relation to our inability to know. Often what is at issue is not just not-knowing but the impossibility of knowing. The association of knowledge with potential danger is based on a profoundly anti-humanist intellectual outlook. In this model, knowledge and science are both limited in their grasp of the truth; and because they set in motion innovations that have unintended effects, they also create problems. Such an outlook is, of course, strongly shaped by the negative experience of political change in the twentieth century. The failure of political experimentation in the Soviet Union and China, disappointment with the record of the Welfare State and disenchantment with the promise of the Enlightenment is interpreted as direct proof that ambitious political programmes do not work; and, retrospectively, such negative experiences confirm that we simply do not know how to know. Thus, the authority of knowledge is further devalued.

The preoccupation with uncertainty and risk does not explicitly lead to the rejection of knowledge. Rather, it helps to consolidate a mood that assigns to knowledge an essentially defensive role. From this precautionary perspective, knowledge is required to accommodate to the prevailing climate of uncertainty and anxiety. The sense of powerlessness with which change is perceived has weakened people's belief in the possibility of knowing what lies ahead, reflected in the demand that 'science must not run ahead of public opinion', and the notion that the ethos of precaution must dictate the pace at which knowledge develops. The development of knowledge has always been subject to pragmatic concerns, but today such concerns have a distinctly defensive focus. And because the authority of knowledge has been compromised through experience, the argument that it should be allowed to be pursued for its own sake carries less conviction then in previous times.

Relativism: the contestation of knowledge claims

The sense of powerlessness in the face of uncertainty is reinforced by the sentiment that meaning and truth elude our grasp. In turn, the disorientation and anxiety bred by uncertainty has helped foster a mood that is hospitable to the ceaseless questioning of knowledge and truth. Such reactions readily converge with the anti-Enlightenment disdain for the idea of universalistic truths. In the nineteenth century, the project of relativizing knowledge was designed to shield tradition against the claims of universalism. Cultural relativism sought to protect religion and traditional morality and values against what was perceived as the threat posed by science, objective truths and universal values. According to opponents of the Enlightenment, different communities had a particular way of making sense of the world, and their values were the product of their own specific circumstances. It was claimed that each of these particular perspectives was of equal validity and provided far more insight into the ways of the world than the so-called abstract universalism of the Enlightenment.

Since the 1960s, cultural relativism has succeeded in becoming a powerful intellectual force. Disenchantment with the Enlightenment tradition has encouraged many thinkers and sections of the public to make sense of their lives through particularistic perspectives. The caricatured version of universalism upheld by the institutions of Western society proved to be no match to the powerful spirit of disenchantment that prevailed in the second half of the twentieth century.[12] One consequence of this process was to put the authority of objective truth on the defensive – and thereby putting to question all truth claims.

Whereas in the past the most systematic critique of universalism was mounted by the right, today, by contrast, the

---

[12] This argument is developed at length in Furedi (1992).

cultural left is its most aggressive opponent. Since the late eighteenth century, concepts such as reason, progress and universalism have been generally associated with the left. But, since the 1960s, the New Left has begun a systematic demolition of those values, by questioning the claims of reason, progress and universalism. The new philosophical posture was reflected in the political approach that acclaimed diversity and opposed universalistic values.[13] Unlike the nineteenth-century critics of the Enlightenment, the New Left was not, in its origin, motivated by a conservative impulse to defend tradition. But because Western capitalism presented its values as universal, the New Left unthinkingly became opposed to it. The New Left not only rejected universalism in general, it adopted a particularistic world-view linked to the politics of identity. Unconsciously, the New Left reaction to postwar Western capitalism internalized the methods and arguments of the conservative reaction to the Enlightenment.

During the 1960s, the left's love affair with relativism was hesitant and semi-conscious, but by the late 1970s, radical intellectuals and, more often, ex-radicals were speaking the language of Nietzsche. In a process aptly described by Alan Bloom as the 'Nietzscheanization of the Left', the left, repelled by modernism, took a cultural turn towards particularism, heterogeneity and difference. It is worth recalling that the original methodological orientation towards difference began as the defence of aristocratic and ruling-class privilege. Differences in moral and mental capacities were advanced to account for and legitimize the social hierarchy. By the mid-nineteenth century, this perspective attached itself to racial differences and helped to legitimize the notion that there was a global hierarchy of people. The cultural left did not set out, as the Social Darwinist did, to provide intellectual sustenance to racial superiority. But the

---

[13] For a discussion of this development, see Furedi (1992), chapter 8.

conservative potential of a particularistic doctrine has crystallized into the cultural left's suspicion of cosmopolitan and global trends. As the rebellion against the rhetoric of universalism turned into a celebration of difference, the process of intellectual de-radicalization became inescapable. The outcome has been the ascendancy of what is called postmodernism and its systematic repudiation of objective knowledge.

Today's postmodernists follow the path set out by the anti-Enlightenment reaction of the nineteenth century. They claim that all knowledge is socially constructed; therefore, all knowledges are incommensurable and all knowledges are in principle, equally valid. Truth depends entirely on the perspective adopted. Postmodernists frequently claim that there is no single road to understanding. This insistence on difference also pertains to methodology – truths are arrived at by different methods. The elaboration of the relativization of methodology is one of the distinctive characteristics of postmodernism. It is based on the old romantic conviction that the road to understanding is through subjectivity, specifically intuition. Postmodernists have elaborated this idea to suggest that since there are many truths, there are also many valid ways of getting there. It is also suggested that those who live a particular experience are best capable of understanding it. Some would claim they are the *only* ones fit to comment on their particular experience.

The elaboration of methodological relativism is rarely made explicit. In general, it assumes the polemical form of an accusation of cultural imperialism or ethnocentrism. For example, in the United States it has been strongly suggested that only blacks have the right to write black history. During the past three decades a number of groups have taken out a patent on their soul, and their unique way of knowing becomes the validation of their knowledge. Of all groups, academic feminism has the most elaborated particularistic epistemology. In reaction to an apparently male-centred world-view, some cultural feminists try to project a female-centred one. Carole Gilligan's *A Woman's Way of Knowing* clearly expresses the trend towards the marriage of subjective experience and knowledge. Moreover, as Novick writes, 'for many feminists the ideology of "difference" extended to fundamental questions of cognitive style and epistemological values'.[14]

Specific female qualities are abstracted by feminist theorists to elaborate women's perspective. Needless to say, from this exclusivist cultural point of view only women can know women. Novick reminds us that by the 'late 1970s the assertion that women's history could only be legitimately written from a feminist standpoint was no longer argued; it was a settled question, beyond argument'.[15]

The denunciation of 'Western rationality' or 'male logic' assumes that theorizing and knowing is to be equated with experiencing. This perspective contends that the path to the truth is above all through subjective experience rather than theorizing or contemplating. Yet being black or white or male or female or disabled or Japanese does not confer a privileged access to the knowledge of the experience. As Mattick persuasively argues, being part of a culture does not give the individual greater understanding of that culture than those who study it from the outside. He writes that 'participants in a culture, even while they may (and indeed must) know the rules and criteria regulating social behaviour in that culture, may have only a very vague notion of how the parts of social life in which they participate fit together'. To strengthen his point, Mattick cites Fritz Machlup's illustration of an alien Martian anthropologist who observes the stock market and interviews its participants:

Since probably 999 out of 1000 persons on the stock market do not really know what it does and how it does it, the most

14 See Novick (1988), p. 494.
15 See Novick (1988), p. 496.

diligent observer-plus-interviewer would remain largely ignorant. Alas, economics cannot be learned either by watching or by interviewing the people engaged in economic activities. It takes a good deal of theorizing before one can grasp the complex interrelations in an economic system.[16]

Observation, like experience, is meaningless outside the framework of a theory. The precondition for a sound account of how the stock exchange works is not contingent on being employed there. Someone with the possession of a sound theory of economic life is far more likely to grasp the intricate workings of the stock market.

The tendency to equate knowledge with the insights that people gain from fragmentary experience makes it impossible to have a meaningful common standard to evaluate knowledge claims. Through transforming knowledge into knowledges, the role of the intellectual has become compromised. The knowledge possessed by the intellectual can be interpreted as just a point of view with no special significance for society. It is not only the role of the intellectual that has been affected by this trend. The growing trend towards the relativization of knowledge claims has had a significant impact on pedagogic theories and practice. Many educationalists now regard experiential learning as having a status comparable to theoretical knowledge

The doctrine of cultural relativism has contributed to the flourishing of pedagogic theories that encourage a philistine attitude towards knowledge. Today, the postmodern influence on education theory has become widespread. Its suspicion towards universal standards is recycled in schools through criticizing systems of assessment based on a common standard. Some postmodern educationalists argue that knowledge itself – rationality and objectivity is merely a male prejudice. Dale

[16] Mattick (1986), p. 32.

Spender and Elizabeth Sarah argue that male experts have constructed 'educational knowledge' so as to control who passes and who fails. In place of 'educational knowledge', these influential critics call for the recognition of 'personal knowledge'. They argue that 'everyone has a personal knowledge which is valid and there is no way of classifying this'.[17] In schools, the subjective experience of children has been endowed with considerable authority. From this perspective, the role assigned to teachers is not to teach knowledge that is external to this experience, but to cultivate and bring out insights that the child already possesses. As one critic of this development argues: 'the redefinition of knowledge as the subjective experience of the child has entailed a shift in emphasis from teacher to learner'.[18] The celebration of children's particular experience is systematically pursued in school textbooks, which are dominated by the ethos of relevance. It appears that children must not be confronted with images and ideas that are alien to their experience. In subjects like history and literature, classical stories are helpfully 'updated' in order to help children understand them.

But what exactly is personal knowledge? It is what children learn through their personal experience. For children, personal knowledge is what they learn at home, from their peers and from the media. Such personal knowledge provides children with valuable insights about the world but does not provide them with the education that enables them to question, conceptualize, problem-solve and to develop intellectually. The equation of 'personal knowledge 'with 'educational knowledge' fails to distinguish between the arbitrary experience of a child and the systematic attempt to develop his or her potential.

But it is in the university system where the line that divides knowledge from everyday insight has become most blurred.

---

[17] Spender and Sarah (1992), p. 42.
[18] Phillips (1998), pp. 48–9.

Advocates of wider participation often attempt to weaken the authority of intellectual knowledge in order to facilitate access to higher education. This approach is justified on the grounds that it is a student-based, rather than a subject-based, approach to learning. One of the ways that advocates of this policy seek to realize their objective is through the accreditation of prior learning, where students are effectively rewarded for learning about their experiences of life before arriving at university. From this perspective, the insights gained through the banal routine of daily existence are qualitatively similar to the knowledge gained through systematic study.

Support for recognizing 'personal knowledge' is not confined to postmodernist theorists. The government exam boards and many universities all now accept accreditation of prior knowledge as a useful assessment tool. Personal experience is given academic credence and homemakers are accepted on courses because their life experiences of budget planning, organizational skills and communicating are represented as the equivalent of a Communication Studies A level. One advocate of accrediting prior learning explains the approach in the following terms:

> The justification normally given for thus using experiential learning is based on the assumption that people have learnt and continue to learn through their life and work experience. They bring this learning with them to higher education and therefore it can be recognized through appropriate assessment. This involves systematizing it in terms of specific knowledge and skills, a process that is thought to require reflection. In effect the raw material of subjective experience is transformed into 'objective' statements of learning outcomes.[19]

Lessons learnt through the school of life are recycled as

[19] Robin Usher, 'Qualification, Paradigms and Experimental Learning in Higher Education', in Fulton (1989), p. 65.

knowledge through the administrative process of subjecting them to learning outcomes. If this process simply involved another small dose of credentialism, there would be little need to remark on it. But the very process of assigning authority to prior learning devalues the authority of real knowledge. The lessons of life may be interesting and pertinent to the individual concerned but, even at their best, reflections on individual experience are far too arbitrary, specific and personal to generate knowledge that can give meaning and understanding to people in society. Knowledge is often produced through detaching people from their immediate experience, so that they can transcend their specific circumstances and through their position of detachment learn to appropriate the insights generated by society as a whole.

The devaluation of the authority of knowledge is not an accidental side effect of the crusade to accredit prior learning. Those who support the cause of the 'access movement' do not hold in high regard the knowledge gained through systematic study, research and experimentation. They believe not only that this knowledge is just a social construction, but that it is used to reinforce elitist privilege. This view is particularly hostile to the authority of pure research, since 'it occupies a privileged position and is an important determinant of status, the distribution of resources and general attitudes and orientations'. In addition it 'contributes to exclusivity on the grounds of the need to maintain the highest "standards" of research and relegates student-centred provision to a lower priority'.[20] Since the product of pure research is not easily accessible to most people, those who embrace the dogma of access regard it merely as an elitist obstacle that stands in the way of the realization of their cause. That is why they can so readily dismiss the hard-earned intellectual achievements of human civilization and why they

[20] Robin Usher, 'Qualification, Paradigms and Experiential Learning in Higher Education', in Fulton (1989), p. 75.

continually scorn 'standards' as something of an elitist confidence trick.

The higher education establishment has accepted the restricted status assigned to intellectual knowledge. It has done so through treating as knowledge every outcome of a learning experience. Academia has accepted that subjective emotional insights and skills-based training should be labelled 'knowledges', while accreditation of prior learning puts life skills on a par with academic qualifications, and work-related training and vocationalism on a par with scholarship. As Ron Barnett argues in his book *Realizing the University*, 'process knowledge, tacit knowledge, action learning, experiential learning: all these terms point to the multiplication of our ways of knowing in the modern world'. The multiplication of different ways of knowing deprives intellectual knowledge of any unique significance. Why bother to work hard to learn, when you can pick up a bit of experiential learning in the bar and gain formal accreditation for it?

The student-centred perspective, like other forms of the relativist world-view, continually attempts to confine knowledge to that which emerges from a particular experience. Its hostility to intellectual knowledge that transcends particularity is fuelled by the realization that its own status and authority depends on discrediting knowledge with a capital K. Its success is shown by the influence it has gained over the education establishment and its institutions. In or out of these institutions, objective knowledge does not enjoy a powerful cultural validation.

Instrumentalist compromise

Despite the intensification of trends that attempt to restrain the authority of knowledge, society continues to need insights in order to deal with the complex problems thrown up in our uncertain world. The culture of fear that influences the public's apprehension of technological innovation and experimentation coexists with the demand for more science and more knowledge of the workings of the natural world. Similarly, cultural relativism may thrive on campuses and in the arts and the media, but government and business are continually looking for objective knowledge to settle many of the disputes facing society. Pragmatism and the pressure to compete and solve new challenges ensures that there is a thriving market for objective knowledge.

Cardinal Newman, in his nineteenth-century classic defence of the liberal university, *The Idea of a University*, observed that 'Knowledge is capable of being its own end'. This idea of knowledge for its own end has seldom been realized in practice. Universities and other institutions have always been forced to engage with the pressures of conflicting interests and practical matters. Although there is a relationship of tension, the valuing of knowledge and being interested in its application can live alongside one another. Pure and applied research, and abstract and empirical theory, can thrive so long as the authority of knowledge is accepted in society. The problem today is not the pragmatic demand for practical knowledge. It is that instrumentalist pressures on knowledge production are rarely contained by a wider quest for understanding.

Instrumentalist pressure on knowledge production happily coexists with the regressive trends discussed above. Private business, government, the media and the university have internalized the mood of scepticism towards the legacy of the enlightenment. They have assimilated the precautionary attitude towards the development of knowledge and given way to the influence of relativism, especially upon culture and politics. An informal compromise has been established whereby knowledge can develop where it is practically necessary. This has led to the emergence of an uneasy coexistence of competing knowledge claims. As a result, producers of knowledge need to share cultural authority with groups who are in the business of restraining the development of reason and science.

Of course people still contribute to the development of knowledge. But in a world where knowledge production is entirely driven by pragmatic concerns, we have become devoid of the ability to decide collectively how to value and how to affirm knowledge. Without meaning, knowledge becomes less the property of the public than of the specialist, the disciplinarian and the expert. The fragmentation of intellectual life leading to the proliferation of specialisms is not simply a response to the need to engage with a complex world. The growth of specialization is fuelled by a culture where intellectuals are discouraged from looking at the big picture, and encouraged to find meaning in their specialty. Discussions are increasingly self-referential and not designed to communicate and engage people outside a specific field of speciality. In such circumstances, objective knowledge appears to have a technical character, and experts and technicians displace those searching for more profound insights. Instead of Knowledge we have developed the tendency to develop micro-knowledge.

One problem with the new group of experts, specialists and knowledge brokers is that their insights are limited to their speciality. Moreover there is no cultural support for the project of transforming those insights into a wider public discourse. Yet reality is multidimensional, and its knowledge demands that we can talk and work across disciplines and specialisms. Unfortunately even in the university, the imperative of specialization mitigates against the acquisition of the general knowledge that is a prerequisite for the functioning of a genuinely knowledge-oriented society. Ultimately the erosion of knowledge with a capital K serves to deprive society of a wider web of common meaning.

The strong cultural pressures that have promoted the feeble version of knowledge that prevails today encourage a philistine attitude towards the life of the mind. Pragmatism towards the use of knowledge can limit the damage caused by the trends discussed above. But pragmatism itself diverts intellectual energies away from realizing the potential for making a significant impact on public life, towards an obsession with narrow specialization.

3   Dumbing Down

The devaluation of the status of the intellectual and the authority of knowledge has important implications for the conduct of public life. Intellectuals in the early twenty-first century have a modest input into public debate, and the public is certainly not preoccupied with a battle of ideas. Moreover, the subordination of knowledge to pragmatic objectives has helped foster an intellectual mood that is inhospitable to experimentation and the development of powerful ideas. The displacement of the thinker by the expert has also weakened the public's interest in debating big issues. In this climate intellectuals find it difficult both to find their voice and to find an audience. As Pierre Hassner remarked, 'in the West, as in the East, not only do public intellectuals find it hard to get a hearing, but it is not certain that they have something to say'.[1]

Philistinism in the domain of culture has been paralleled by similar trends influencing public debate and political life. One of the clearest manifestations of this process is the manifest decline in the standards of political debate. Spoon-feeding the public with sound bites has become a highly prized political skill. Professional speech-writers pursue their task as if their audience was composed of easily distracted children and, not surprisingly, political discussion tends to be shallow, short-termist and bereft of ideas. This is the age of 'micro-politics', where, in Britain at

---

[1]   Pierre Hassner, 'The Public Intellectual and the Experience of Totalitarianism', in Melzer *et al.* (2003), p. 138.

least, politics presents itself through the depoliticized language of managerialism, technocracy and business. Politicians promise to 'deliver', and claim that their policies add 'value' or are 'value for money'. Policies are no longer good – they are 'evidence-based'. Policies are rarely generated by a world-view – they are derived from 'best practice'. New Labour's Third Way-speak is entirely devoted to managerial process talk that promises 'transparency' and 'accountability'.

In the United States, the level of political rhetoric is indeed designed for adults who are seen to have the mental capacity of children. A disturbing study of presidential debates carried out by *The Princeton Review* analysed transcripts of the Gore–Bush debates, the Clinton–Bush–Perot debate of 1992, the Kennedy–Nixon debate of 1960, and the Lincoln–Douglas debate of 1858. It reviewed these transcripts using a standard vocabulary test that indicates the minimum educational standard needed for a reader to grasp the text. According to the analysis, during the debates of 2000, Bush spoke at a sixth-grade level (6.7) and Gore at a high seventh-grade level (7.9). In 1992, Clinton achieved a seventh-grade standard (7.6), Bush managed to achieve a sixth-grade level (6.8) as did Perot (6.3). Their contribution compares poorly with the Kennedy–Nixon exchange, where both candidates used language appropriate for tenth-graders. In turn, their achievement appears feeble compared to that of Abraham Lincoln and Stephen Douglas, whose scores were, respectively, 11.2 and 12.0.[2] No doubt sections of today's cultural elite would interpret the decline of oratory since the nineteenth century as, on balance, a positive development. In today's political rhetoric George W. Bush's sixth-grade language is obviously more 'inclusive' and less 'elitist' than that of Abraham Lincoln. But this inclusive language is symptomatic of a general tendency to treat the public as if they

[2] See Diane Ravitch, 'Dumbing Down the Public: Why It Matters', in *Reason*, April 2001.

were not capable of understanding arguments that would test the mental capacities of a precocious ten-year-old child.

Political rhetoric in the UK is also becoming a lost art. During the 2003 party conference season, the leaders of the main parties reached a new low in the content of their speeches. Iain Duncan Smith, the leader of the Conservative Party, attempted to imitate an angry thirteen-year-old arguing with his friends in the playground. The main focus of his conference speech was repeatedly to call Tony Blair a 'liar'. For his part, Tony Blair's conference oration was so vacuous that several people who were in the audience told me that they simply could not remember what he said.

The tendency to patronize the public is sometimes presented as an attempt to connect with people who simply lack the education necessary to understand complex ideas. However, this argument fails to explain why similar trends are also evident in institutions that are devoted to the promotion of arts, culture and education. Whatever the complex reasons behind the self-conscious dumbing down of politics, its impact on the public is all too evident. A public which is continuously spoon-fed platitudes and sound bites is likely to become estranged from the world of political debate. This development is particularly striking on university campuses, where students continually insist that 'politics is boring'. The language used on campuses reflects an intense sense of cynicism towards causes and ideas, and a distinct lack of interest in holding strong views of any sort. *New York Times* journalist Michiko Kakutani's reflection on the language used by American college students captures this mood of disengagement. 'That familiar interjection "whatever" says a lot about the state of mind of college students today', notes Kakutani. He adds: 'so do the catch phrases "no problem", "not even" and "don't go there" '.[3] With such little importance attached to ideas, intel-

---

[3]   Michiko Kakutani, 'Debate? Dissent? Discussion? Oh, Don't Go There!', *New York Times*, 23 March 2002.

lectual argument has acquired negative connotations. Scholars who pursue their points with vigour can now be accused of 'academic bullying'. British universities encourage academics to ban an 'adversarial' style of debate from the seminar rooms and provide a 'supportive environment' for students. A strong argument has been redefined as a form of mental intimidation. Such attitudes are even more in evidence on American campuses. 'Debate has gotten a very bad name in our culture', notes Jeff Nunokawa, a professor of English at Princeton University. '[I]t's become synonymous with some of the most non-intellectual forms of bullying, rather than as an opportunity for deliberative democracy.'[4]

Given the extent to which the authority of knowledge has been devalued, the negative connotations acquired by conflict of opinion and heated debate are entirely understandable. With so little at stake, what's the point of arguing? If ideas have such little consequence, insistence on one's point of view appears as pig-headedness and bad manners. Criticizing someone else's ideas is readily interpreted as ego-tripping or as an act of insensitivity, while the very act of questioning someone's view can appear as a personal insult. 'It's as though there's no distinction between the person and the argument, as though to criticize an argument would be injurious to the person', observes Amanda Anderson, an English professor at Johns Hopkins University.[5] The mood of relativism, discussed in the previous chapter, reinforces the belief that insisting on the validity of an idea is a form of bad manners. If all perspectives have validity, then differences cannot be resolved through debate. 'That is your view' is the perfectly acceptable response to criticism – and a clear statement that ratifies the pointlessness of further discussion.

---

[4] Cited in Michiko Kakutani, 'Debate? Dissent? Discussion? Oh, Don't Go There!', 23 March 2002.

[5] Cited in Michiko Kakutani, 'Debate? Dissent? Discussion? Oh, Don't Go There!', 23 March 2002.

The powerful influence of relativist currents has made it difficult to debate matters of substance. As Russell Berman and Stephen Haber argue, 'the shared beliefs that allowed debate to take place have now largely been eroded'.[6] Without a common intellectual language and a minimalist consensus about standards, real debate becomes difficult to conduct.

The estrangement of academia from the intense and creative experience of debates that have consequences has encouraged a cultural style that celebrates intellectual disengagement. Public debate, controversy and the single-minded pursuit of ideas, once seen as fundamental features of academic life, are no longer accorded automatic respect. Academic freedom is no longer an inviolable right that people are prepared to defend. Traditionally academics, particularly social scientists, have been in the forefront of asserting the principle of freedom of speech. These days academics attempt to deny their colleagues the right to free speech. The campaign to ban Tom Paulin from speaking at Harvard for being anti-Semitic, and the censoring of Israeli academics by the editor of an academic journal based in Manchester on the grounds that they are Israeli, is a testimony to the illiberal tendencies that prevail in academia.

Academic freedom has become negotiable. In the US there has been little opposition to the introduction of campus speech codes that prohibit speech that 'offends'. In the UK, academics have barely raised a murmur about the introduction of processes and regulations that compromise the free pursuit of knowledge and research. Lecturers now need to ensure that their teaching is consistent with bureaucratically devised 'learning outcomes' that meet the requirements of externally imposed benchmarking criteria. Lecturers are no longer supposed to teach what they think needs to be taught, and they certainly do not have the right

---

[6]   Russell Berman and Stephen Haber, 'Whatever happened to the Academic left?', *Hoover Digest*, 2002, no. 2.

to lecture material for which the learning outcome cannot be demonstrated in advance. Fortunately, despite these formalities, scholars still teach what they think they should teach, but the acceptance of these bureaucratic codes underlines the fragile foundation for academic freedom.

Of course words can offend. But one of the roles of a university is to question conventional truths. The pursuit of ideas has always demanded that intellectuals question the sacred and mention the unmentionable. A civilized intellectual institution teaches its members how *not* to take criticisms personally, and how *not* to be offended by uncomfortable ideas. It also teaches its members how to deal with being offended.

Cavalier attitudes towards free and unfettered debate, and lack of enthusiasm for engagement in controversy, contribute towards the wider sense of political malaise. Instead of countering the public's mood of disengagement, such attitudes provide cultural affirmation for it. The absence of a cultural commitment to debate does not cause the disengagement of the public from the political process, but these two things are inextricably linked. More importantly, the diminishing status of debate underlines the lack of respect that society accords to intellectual clarification.

A disengaged public

Politicians have come to recognize that their political, ideological and moral links with the electorate are fragile. Traditional forms of party politics, political values and identities have little purchase on an evidently disenchanted public. Popular mistrust of authority is confirmed by the growing alienation of people from the system of elections. American-style voting apathy has become a fact of life in the New Europe, where a significant proportion of the electorate believes that voting is a waste of time. The low turnout of voters affects the authority of governments who are keenly sensitive to the erosion of their legitimacy. Unfortunately, the predominant response of politicians is not to seek ways of reconnecting with the public but to avoid the problem through looking for quick-fix solutions.

Increasingly, every election threatens to become an embarrassing reminder of the political wasteland that we inhabit. Apathy is no longer an adequate term of description for the steady erosion of the public's involvement in the political life of the United States. In almost every presidential election since 1960, voter participation has steadily declined – from 62.5 per cent of the electorate in 1960 to 50.1 per cent in 1988. During the election in 1996, only 49 per cent of the voting-age population bothered to cast their ballots – the lowest turn out since 1924. The election in 2000 continued this pattern, with only about 50 per cent of registered voters participating. The alienation of the public from the political process is particularly striking in relation to the election of 2000. Unlike the election of 1996, where the outcome was seen to be a foregone conclusion, the contest in 2000 was the most open for decades. Yet the number of Americans who voted was roughly the same as in 1996. According to the Committee for the Study of the American Electorate, the cumulative effect of voter disengagement during the past 30 years is that today, '25 million Americans who used to vote no longer do so'. Yet voter participation in presidential elections appears positively high compared to the ballots cast for candidates running for a seat in the House of Representatives. These have averaged around 35 per cent in the 1990s.

In the aftermath of 9/11, media pundits speculated that this tragic event and the sense of patriotism to which it gave rise might increase political participation. However, it soon became evident that not even such a major event could disrupt the pre-existing pattern of disengagement. The first 18 primaries prior to 5 July 2002 saw 'not just low turnout, but record low turnout –

with only eight per cent of Democrats and seven per cent of Republicans going to the polls'.[7]

Nor can European commentators feel smug about the political illiteracy of the American electorate. In Britain, the facts speak for themselves. It is worth recalling that back in 1997, New Labour was backed by only 31 per cent of those qualified to vote. Voter turnout at this election was the lowest since 1945. Even the much-hyped public relations campaign surrounding devolution in Scotland and Wales failed to engage the public's interest. Voter participation in these 'history-making' elections in 1999 indicated that the public regarded devolution as another stage-managed event. Only 46 per cent of the Welsh electorate voted, while in Scotland, a high-profile media campaign designed to promote voter participation led to a turnout of 59 per cent, less than two thirds. On the same day, polling booths in England were empty, with only 29 per cent of registered voters turning out for the 6 May local elections. The June 1999 UK elections to the European Parliament brought a turnout of 23 per cent – and in one Sunderland polling station, only 15 people turned up out of the 1000 entitled to vote. In the 2001 General Election, apathy emerged as the dominant issue under debate – and the turnout was an all-time low of 59 per cent. Tony Blair was returned to office with the backing of just 24 per cent of the electorate.

The Brent East by-election in September 2003 is symptomatic of the process of political disengagement. After the Liberal Democrats managed to win this traditional Labour seat, the result was characterized as a 'political earthquake' and the 'biggest hammer blow of Tony Blair's political career'. A closer inspection of this event reveals that this so-called earthquake was produced by a combination of low turnout and voters' cynicism with the government. On a turnout of 36 per cent this was one of the most disengaged high-profile by-elections in British politics.

---

[7]   See Seth Gitell, 'Apathy at the polls', *The Boston Phoenix*, 4 December 2002.

Apathy and disengagement breed both anti-political and apolitical reactions. The political class is aware of this: but instead of attempting to address the underlying malaise and disillusionment through developing challenging political ideals that could inspire the electorate to vote, its response has been to acquiesce in dumbing down. The recall of Governor Gray Davis, and the resulting election of Arnold Schwarzenegger to the governorship of California in 2003, is a testimony to the triumph of political illiteracy in the Anglo-American world. This event was not simply the triumph of personality over politics but the outcome of the inexorable decline of the authority of ideals. Arnie personifies the anti-politician politician, who makes no claims to stand for anything. This recall election may appear as a typically Californian event that could not happen in Europe, but as the French newspaper *Le Figaro* reminded its readers: 'You shouldn't mock Arnold Schwarzenegger; what California invents, America adopts and Europe ends up imitating.'[8]

The steady decline of voter participation is directly linked to a much wider process. Lack of participation provides a clear index of disillusionment and public mistrust in the existing political system. Surveys of American public attitudes indicate that approval of the government has steadily declined in recent decades. Whereas in 1958, over 75 per cent of the American people trusted their government to do the right thing, only 28.2 per cent could express a similar sentiment in 1990. Since the beginning of this decade, trust in politicians has continued to decline. The 1996 survey conducted by Gallup, titled 'In a State of Disunion', found that 64 per cent of the respondents had little or no confidence that government officials tell the truth.

A major study carried out by the Brookings Institution in May 2002 found that not even the wave of patriotism that followed in the aftermath of 9/11 translated into a durable

---

[8]   *Le Figaro*, 7 October 2003.

growth of trust in the US government. This survey showed that whereas in July 2001 only 29 per cent of Americans expressed a positive regard for their government, this figure almost doubled to 57 per cent in the aftermath of 11 September 2001. However, by May 2002, public trust in federal government had fallen back to 40 per cent, and experts felt that the opportunity for the reforging of a relationship of trust had already probably passed.[9]

Surveys in Europe point to a similar pattern. Studies carried out in the European Union indicate that around 45 per cent of the population is dissatisfied with the 'way that democracy works'. In Britain, surveys reveal a high level of public cynicism towards politicians. A Gallup poll conducted in April 1995 concluded that most people's opinion of Members of Parliament was 'low' or 'very low'. A decade previously, only a third of people adopted this view. According to another survey, carried out in 1994, only 24 per cent of the population believed that the British government places the national interest above their party interests.[10] Politicians consistently come at the bottom of the list of professions that the public trusts. A survey published by the ICM in June 1999 found that only 10 per cent of the respondents stated that they trust politicians a lot, 65 per cent a little, and 25 per cent not at all.[11] A study carried out by the BBC in February 2002 indicated that many people under the age of 45 regarded politicians as 'crooks', 'liars' and a 'waste of time'.[12]

During the 1990s, the erosion of public trust was reflected in a national mood of suspicion towards the political system itself. What emerged was a brand of anti-politics, a cynical dismissal of the elected politician and an obsession with sleaze and corruption

[9] Mackenzie and Labiner (2001), pp. 2–3.
[10] J. Curtice and R. Jowell, 'The sceptical electorate', in Jowell, Curtice, Park, Brook and Ahrendt (1995), pp. 141 and 148.
[11] Findings of the poll published in the *Guardian*, 8 June 1999.
[12] 'Politics a "turn-off" for under 45s', *BBC News*, 28 February 2002.

in Westminster and Washington. The Clinton era was one of
permanent scandal; and controversy surrounded the manner of
Bush's election, only to be followed by a series of corporate
scandals culminating in the Enron collapse. New Labour's success
at portraying the Conservatives as a party of sleaze was crucial to
its electoral success of 1997 – but the New Labour government
quickly found that it was not immune to the politics of scandal. A
spate of minor scandals involving Labour MPs and ministers
followed the 1997 election victory, and the issue of sleaze
continued to haunt the government through 1998, as successive
ministers were forced to resign. The furore that surrounded
Cheriegate in December 2002 – despite the absence of any
allegation that the Prime Minister's wife had done anything
illegal – indicates that cynicism towards government is a
permanent feature of life.

The exhaustion of political life has little to do with political
corruption, inept political leaders or insensitive bureaucracies.
What has changed during the past two decades is the very
meaning of politics itself. At the beginning of the twentieth
century, political life was dominated by radically different
alternatives. Competing political philosophies offered contrasting
visions of the good society. Conflict between these ideologies was
often fierce and sometimes provoked violent clashes, even
revolutions. 'Left' and 'Right' were no mere labels. In a
fundamental sense, they endowed individuals with an identity
that said something very important about how they regarded
their lives. Ardent advocates of revolutionary change clashed
with fervent defenders of the capitalist system, and these
competing views dominated the conduct of everyday politics.

The end of the century offered a radically different political
landscape. Politics today has little in common with the passions
and conflicts that shaped people's commitments and hatreds over
the past century. There is no longer room for either the ardent
defender of the free-market faith, or the robust advocate of

revolutionary transformation. It would be wrong to conclude that politics has become simply more moderate. Politics has gone into early retirement. The big issues of our time – the impending environmental catastrophe, threats to our health, killer bugs, weapons of mass destruction – are presented as perils that stand above politics. It is widely believed that the world is out of control and that there is little that human beings can do to master these developments or influence their destiny. Deprived of choice and options, humanity is forced to acquiesce in a world-view that Margaret Thatcher aptly described as TINA – There Is No Alternative.

If indeed there is no alternative, politics can have little meaning. Without alternatives, debate becomes empty posturing about trivial matters. Politicians are forced to inflate relatively banal proposals to the level of a major policy innovation. This is the age of 'micro-politics', in which politics has adopted the language of technocracy and presents itself through a depoliticized language of managerialism. The growth of a managerial political style has gone hand-in-hand with a shift to the personal. Even protest movements have internalized a highly individualistic and personal style of political vocabulary. 'Not In My Name', the prominent slogan of demonstrators against the 2003 Iraq war, is a statement of personal preference. It does not even purport to engage or convince other people. Not in my name is about me, not you.

Personalities and individual behaviour dominate the presentation of contemporary politics. As public life has become emptied of its content, private and personal preoccupations have been projected into the public sphere. Consequently, passions that were once stirred by ideological differences are far more likely to be engaged by individual misbehaviour, private troubles and personality conflicts. The private lives of politicians excite greater interest than the way they handle their public office. In Britain it is widely noted that the reality TV show *Big Brother* 'arouses passions that politics can no longer stir'.[13] In the US, a television programme titled *The American Candidate* aims to use the reality TV format to pick a 'people's candidate' from its contestants. This format is being adopted in the UK and is likely to be transmitted before the next general election. With so many people turned off managerial politics, is it any surprise that politicians are turning to reality television producers, to learn how to engage with an uninterested public?

Re-engagement through the lowest common denominator

The disengagement of people from the institutions of society is the defining feature of contemporary political life. It is also the principal problem that preoccupies the energies of the political establishment and the cultural elite. Sadly, these groups have drawn the conclusion that apathy and cynicism are responses to a political culture that is too sophisticated and too challenging for ordinary people. From this standpoint, the political elites have drawn the conclusion that the way to re-engage is to be less demanding and less challenging. What is often called the *politics of inclusion* is a project that is designed to bypass the problem, by demanding very little of people, and seeking a technical quick-fix for the political malaise.

Instead of being concerned with the lack of substance of contemporary politics, the cultural elite believes that the way to reconnect with the public is through dumbing down further. This attitude informs the various projects that are designed to contain the problem of low voter turnout. Instead of attempting to improve the standard of political discourse or encourage involvement through debate, politicians and officials seek to

---

[13] See Alice Thomson, 'Politics doesn't have to be like the *Big Brother* House', *Daily Telegraph*, 4 December 2002.

make voting as easy and effortless as possible. This project is justified by the dubious assumption that the reason why people don't vote is because they are very busy or because people find the exercise a difficult one. Instead of acknowledging the fact that, for many people, voting is now seen as a pointless effort, there is a tendency to complicate matters by suggesting that electoral participation is a particularly difficult and burdensome task. It appears that travelling to a polling booth, filling in a ballot form and dropping it into a box, is a challenge that severely tests the mental and moral capacity of contemporary adults. So adverts published by Lewisham Council, for the London mayoral election in December 2001, showed a comfortable sofa and a man in a bath, encouraging voters to stay at home and post their ballots. Barry Quirk, chief executive of the Council, advised people to 'simply sit back on the sofa, cast your vote', and added 'it's as easy as that – no more trudging to the polling booth in the rain'.

From the standpoint of democratic ideals, voting involves responsibility and a purposeful intention to make a difference. Today, the ideal that voting implies some kind of a commitment to the democratic process has been subordinated to the pragmatic notion that it should be as effortless an activity as possible. Preferably nothing should be demanded of the voter other than the meaningless act of pushing a button or ticking a box in the comfort of one's home. Predictably, this systematic trivialization of the process of voting is justified on the basis that the electoral process should be as inclusive as possible. Through making a minimal effort, even those who are indifferent to the process can be involved in this caricature of democratic participation. The ideal of the active and interested citizen is increasingly portrayed as a symbol of a bygone elitist era.

At various times, proposals are made to reconnect with the electorate through placing polling booths in supermarkets and other convenient sites, institutionalizing voting via the telephone or the Internet, or text voting, or postal voting. In Britain, electronic voting has been put forward as an instrument for revitalizing the political process. In 2003, e-voting was piloted in English local elections. Predictably, this initiative was proposed on the ground that this was an *inclusive* way forward. Nick Raynsford, the local government minister justified this step in the following terms:

> The electoral pilots aim to improve turnout, in particular among key groups of people who might otherwise be excluded, such as people who are working away from the area, younger voters, the elderly and people with mobility problems.[14]

At a time when very few people believe that there is any point in voting at local elections, the idea that somehow a substantial group of people are 'excluded' by their circumstances is very much the product of the fertile imagination of our cultural elite.

Historical experience demonstrates that when the 'excluded' want to be 'included', they do a very good job of breaking down the barriers to their participation. Restrictions on the right to vote have been swept away by mass movements of workers, women and minority groups. When people believe that voting makes a difference, they rise to the occasion as a politicized public. They do not need electronic solutions that transform the act of voting into a meaningless individualized gesture. As is the case with most initiatives designed to promote inclusion, the object of inclusion is patronized. Just as promoters of inclusion scorn 'elitist' museums, classical education and libraries focused on books, so the advocates of e-voting disparage traditional ways of voting. 'We don't think we can say to people that they can only vote in the traditional way in a rickety booth in a church hall or school using a stubby pencil', declared Raynsford.[15] Through

---

[14] Cited in Simon Parker, 'Cross Culture', *Guardian*, 30 April 2003.
[15] Cited in Simon Parker, 'Cross Culture', *Guardian*, 30 April 2003.

portraying so-called traditional voting as a dreary imposition on the British citizen, Raynsford succeeds in transforming a fundamental feature of democratic life into a burden that no sensible person could tolerate. Voter apathy becomes the fault of cold church halls rather than of the dumbed-down political culture that comes up with such patronizing solutions.

The numerous initiatives dreamt up by the promoters of quick-fix inclusive voting reflect the abandonment of the belief that an active democratic public can be reconstituted. The politics of inclusion is oriented towards the individual rather than a wider section of society. Its various gimmicks – interactivity, postal voting, telephone voting – aim to connect with the people as atomized individuals rather than as an educated public. However, the very individualization of the act of voting deprives it of any meaning. The idea of public duty or communal responsibility is displaced by focusing on individual convenience. Such initiatives can only deactivate, demotivate and further individualize a community. In the May 2000 local elections, the district of Watford in Hertfordshire set up polling booths in shops and permitted the electorate to cast their ballot over the weekend, when fewer would be at work. The outcome? Voter turnout slumped by nearly 10 per cent, to just 27 per cent of the electorate.[16] As an arbitrary, individual act of convenience, the act of voting loses its meaning further still.

Is it any surprise that voting is fast losing its meaning? At a time when the disengagement of the public has become the defining feature of twenty-first-century Western political culture, there are more and more opportunities afforded to people to 'have their say'. Radio and television programmes continually launch new polls. People can vote for their favourite classical record or their favourite pop star. Interactive television and the Internet regularly ask you to have your say about a whole range

---

[16] Cited in Simon Parker, 'Cross Culture', *Guardian*, 30 April 2003.

of issues. The more the act of voting has lost its purpose and meaning, the more desperate attempts are launched to give people yet another opportunity to 'have their say'.

UK commentators have noted, with more than a hint of envy, that more young people vote for their favourite personality on the reality TV programme *Big Brother* than they do in elections. Indeed, it is frequently suggested that politicians have some important lessons to learn from this programme. In a report published by The Hansard Society arguing this point, its author Stephen Coleman, an Oxford academic, observed that politicians need to find exciting ways to use technology to give people more control over how they view the political process. 'The way to liberate political democracy from its current cultural ghetto requires a new conception of two-way accountability; a creative and exciting use of the new technologies of interactivity,' argues Coleman.[17] This techno-fix idea implies that interactivity is in some sense similar to participation and political involvement. From this perspective, children are the easiest to involve – they always want to have their say about their favourite football player or pop star. No wonder numerous British advocacy groups are campaigning to lower the minimum age of voting to 16.

An elitist populism

The tendency to redefine democratic participation using the diffuse notion of 'having your say' is associated with the political agenda of inclusion. This agenda aims to tackle the problem of disengagement through a populist programme that combines flattering people with treating them as children. A project promoting inclusion need have no meaning other than to provide the pretence of participation. That is why the Internet is so often

[17] Cited in '*Big Brother* Gives Politics Lesson', in *BBC News*, 3 June 2003.

held up as the ideal site for participation by the elitist populism of our times. The British author George Walden pointed to the meaningless character of this participation, when he observed: 'of what advantage is it to democracy that from 1998 the Prime Minister could pretend to converse directly with individuals, when in reality all that is happening is that the public's all too predictable complaints are computed by party officials and a pro-forma reply, purporting to come from the PM's mouth, is keyed into the machine?'[18]

In the past, populism was associated with a wider agenda. Today it seems to have no role other than connecting with people. Connecting or interacting has become a substitute for having something to say. Inclusion is its own virtue – it matters little what one is included in. As I argue in Chapter 5, inclusion for its own sake also shapes policies such as widening access to higher education, the arts and culture. Politicians in particular are drawn towards new infantilizing initiatives designed to 'recon-nect' with the public. In Britain, politicians have even consulted Peter Bazalgette, the creator of the reality TV show *Big Brother*, to advise them how to connect with younger voters.

Making do with the pretence of participation reflects the low expectations that the cultural elite has of the public. The Hansard Society's Stephen Coleman believes that politics 'is too closed and obscure for most people' and 'they literally do not understand what is going on'. Behind the populist agenda of inclusion lurks an elitist contempt for people. Often this contempt is most pronounced among liberal or left-wing political activists, who ought to know better. The corollary of the idea that participating needs to be made less demanding is the notion that people are not really up to much. Instead of acknowledging the dearth of political ideas, the public is indicted for being gullible. In the US, this paternalistic impulse led some Democratic Party activists to

[18] Walden (2001), p. 151.

blame the defeat of their presidential candidate in 2000 on the stupidity of the people. One liberal activist, Michael Gronewalter, states that 'civility and intelligent dialogue are useful tools among intelligent people', but are inappropriate for engaging with the public. He argues:

> I really think the problem is that we as liberals are in general far more intelligent, well-reasoned and educated and will go to astonishingly great lengths to convince people of the integrity and validity of our fair and well thought-out arguments. The audience, in case anyone has been paying attention, *isn't always getting it! I suspect the problem is not the speaker – it is most of the audience.*[19]

According to one of Gronewalter's colleagues, the American public has become a sort of 'Fast Food Electorate', and it is as if 'Americans suffer collectively from a plague of Attention Deficit Disorder'. This negative assessment of the American electorate serves to legitimize his call for dumbing down the Democratic message: 'it is time for liberals to use slogans, sound bytes and photo-ops to marry Bush, his administration and his cronies to their corrupt agenda'.[20]

The view that the public is too stupid to grasp the high-minded and sophisticated ideals of American liberals expresses a profound sense of contempt for human beings. Furthermore, it uncritically transfers responsibility for the contemporary malaise of political life on the uneducated electorate. The direct and transparent denunciation of people's mental capacities, made by the activists cited above, is rare in a culture that is at least outwardly anti-elitist. Usually, such contempt is transmitted through nods, winks and terms like '*Daily Mail* reader', 'white

---

[19] Michael Gronewalter, 'Don't Get Smart, Get Stupid', *Democratic Underground.Com*, 13 April 2002.

[20] Christian Dewar, 'Dumbing Down: America's Fast Food Electorate', *Democratic Underground.Com*, 24 April 2002.

van man', 'Mondeo man', 'tabloid readers', 'pebbledash people' and 'Worcester Woman'. In the US the moral superiority of the anti-elitist is affirmed through such terms as 'Nascar dads', 'Valley girls', 'Joe six-pack', 'Redneck', 'dittoheads' or 'salad dodger'. However, what today's cultural elite really thinks of people is most vividly revealed through their attitude towards higher education, culture and other targets of its policy of inclusions. These subjects will be the topics of the following chapters.

4 Social Engineering

Contemporary populism has no wider purpose than to connect with people. Consequently, initiatives designed to increase electoral participation can be entirely indifferent to the intrinsic meaning of the act of voting. Simply pushing a button is sufficient for maintaining the pretence of participation – and if the public lacks the inclination to go to the polling station and vote, for the political elite changing the meaning of voting seems like a small price to pay for maintaining the rate of electoral participation.

The subordination of the democratic act of voting to the objective of retaining contact with people is paralleled throughout cultural life. Nothing seems to have any intrinsic worth. Knowledge, education, higher education, art and culture are not promoted because of any inherent qualities that they may possess. This instrumentalist orientation towards culture is not unprecedented: the commercialization of cultural production has always encouraged an instrumentalist ethos towards intellectual and artistic life. What has changed is that culture is not simply promoted as an economic good, but fervently propagated for advancing the policy of social inclusion. As in the case of voting, culture is valued insofar as it advances the populist agenda of inclusion, participation and access. Increasingly, every aspect of culture is regarded from the standpoint of this agenda. The question is not whether a particular institution or cultural artefact is good or bad, beautiful or ugly, inspiring or uninspiring, but whether it is relevant, accessible or inclusive. Regardless of its content, that which promises to connect with the public can count on the support and affirmation of our cultural elites.

Just as the imperative of social engineering is prepared to change the meaning of voting, so it is ready to endow art, culture, knowledge and the university with a new definition. The imperative to 'connect' leads to a situation where cultural and educational institutions are less likely to be judged according to criteria internal to themselves than on their relevance and accessibility to a wider public. In previous times, so-called High Culture was frequently indicted because it was the monopoly of a small oligarchy and ordinary folk were prevented from enjoying its achievements. Today, the criticism levelled at High Culture is much more likely to take exception to the fact that it is far too demanding to be popular, that it is alien to, and aloof from, people's lives.

Relevance has become a key concept of the contemporary ethos of social engineering. Historically, great thinkers were criticized by populist anti-intellectual demagogues for being out of touch with the needs of the people. The out-of-touch intellectual and artist have been objects of populist derision throughout the past three centuries. Today, this philistine critique has been expanded to embrace any aspect of cultural life that is deemed not directly relevant to the people – which, in practice, means not seen as relevant by policy-makers. Policy-makers and politicians wedded to the imperative of social engineering take great pleasure in attacking major museums and universities for being too stuffy and elitist. Matthew (now Lord) Evans, who was appointed chairman of Resource, the British Government's advisory body on museums, stated in his first major speech in 2000 that museums needed to demonstrate their 'relevance to local communities' by sending their artefacts out to be displayed in shops and pubs.[1] In Britain, smug asides about elitist Oxford

---

[1] Cited in Nigel Reynolds, 'Art elitist? I never meant to say that', *Daily Telegraph*, 16 October 2003. For a discussion of the new philistine trends in the world of museums, see Appleton (2001).

and Cambridge have become a key component of the staple diet of populist politics. It is as if an object exhibited in a pub becomes a focus of praise because it is in a pub, rather than in the National Gallery.

Once values like relevance and accessibility acquire fundamental importance then they become the arbiters of educational and cultural life. From this perspective, the value of a sociological concept, an opera or a Shakespeare play is determined by its relevance and accessibility. And if it fails to be relevant or accessible it may face a populist makeover in order to make it useful to the project of social engineering. In September 2003, it was reported that the Classical Theater Lab in Los Angeles had begun a series of audience-friendly Shakespeare productions. The series 'Who's Afraid of William Shakespeare?' aims to make productions that are not intimidating for the audience. The actors explain the story as they proceed, paraphrase a lot of the difficult language, and stop to answer questions posed by members of the audience.[2]

The simplification of Shakespeare by the Classical Theater Lab is not motivated by any artistic insights that demand a major reinterpretation of the old master's plays. Reinterpretation of a drama fuelled by changing aesthetic sensibility is part and parcel of the evolution of the theatre. However, in this case reinterpretation is not the outcome of an aesthetic judgement, but of the concern to be relevant to the audience. As in the case of e-voting, it is the desire to develop a relationship with the public, rather than the quality of that relationship, that drives the objective of making Shakespeare more digestible.

Certain forms of cultural practices cannot be simplified and made relevant. It is difficult to turn a complex musical symphony, for instance, into family-friendly entertainment. So instead of a populist makeover, it needs to disappear or to be treated with

[2]   John Weeks, 'At last, art for idiots!', in *U-Daily News*, 29 September 2003.

disdain. A clear example of this is the contemporary critique of the essay. According to some advocates of the access movement, the essay is so elitist that you cannot possibly ask ordinary university students to write one. Richard Winter, Professor of Education at Anglia Polytechnic University, argues that essay writing is 'difficult and alien, especially to those returning to formal learning after a substantial break and those who are first-generation participants in higher education'. Winter believes that the essay 'disenfranchises students who may be quite capable of embodying their understanding of ideas in other genres and styles',[3] and that in any case, the essay is overrated and there other, better, ways for students to learn. Winter prefers what he calls 'patchwork' text assignments: small-scale writing tasks designed to make students feel comfortable and confident.

Winter's rejection of the essay in favour of patchwork text assignments reflects the wider tendency of subordinating education and culture to dictates of social inclusion. Predictably, it is not the impulse of education and the cultivation of the mind that drives this approach but something external to it: the politics of inclusion. The call to displace the essay by patchwork text assignments is motivated by the belief that nothing 'alien' should stand between a student and university learning. This declaration has little to do with the essay form itself. But in the course of promoting patchwork texts, Winter cannot help but disparage the worth of the essay. This example indicates that dumbing down is not an accidental by-product of the campaign to widen access to higher education, but the inevitable consequence of a perspective that views the objective of education as something that is external to education. In this case, access and inclusion is the goal and education is the means to achieve it.

A further example of this trend is the current discussion

---

[3] See Richard Winter, 'Regular writing tasks would aid learning far better than the last-minute essay', *Guardian*, 10 June 2003.

around the public library. The Department for Culture, Media and Sport (DCMS) believes that people may be put off going to the library because it looks too much like … a library. One DCMS report speculates that librarians might restrict usage by certain people or sections of the community because of their 'inappropriate attitudes and behaviour', 'inappropriate rules and regulations', or 'book stock policies which do not reflect the needs of the community'. *Better Public Libraries*, a report published by the Commission for Architecture and the Built Environment in August 2003, blames 'traditional notions of the book-lending centres' for a 17 per cent fall in library visits. It demands that libraries should become a 'living room of the city':

> New libraries should increasingly be long-stay places for students, a safe haven for children, even a home from home. They should include cafés, lounge areas with sofas, and chill-out zones where young people can watch MTV, read magazines and listen to CDs on listening posts.[4]

In other words libraries can be involved in the provision of just about any service so long as it is not the tedious business of lending people books. Since getting as many people as possible to walk through the doors of the library is the principal objective, anything that stands in the way of interesting the punters becomes the problem. Books from libraries, like essays from universities, will just have to disappear.

The premise behind *Better Public Libraries* and the policy of access is that any barriers put up by cultural life to people's involvement is a problem to be removed. More broadly, just about any educational or cultural practice that the public does not spontaneously embrace may be stigmatized as elitist. From this perspective, culture is at its best when it can be spoon-fed and

---

[4]   Cited in Martin Wainwright, 'Libraries Blamed for Their Own Decline', *Guardian*, 18 August 2003.

consumed by anyone at any time. But a university discipline, like a cultural practice, has an integrity of its own. And because this endows a book or a painting with its own identity, it necessarily puts up a barrier to spontaneous access. As the British cultural critic Josie Appleton argues, 'anything that has its own identity puts up "barriers" – the fact that it resists you makes you aware that it is a separate object and not your own reflection'. Appleton adds that 'a painting resists the viewer because it has its own logic' and warns 'you can't "get it" immediately when you look at it, you can't take it in in one gulp'.[5]

Appleton's argument also extends to institutions. 'Any institution with any atmosphere at all, such as a library or a museum, is going to put up a kind of "barrier" and will prevent you from feeling as if you are in your living room', she observes. Why? Because a cultural institution has its own sense of itself, its own collection, its own story and integrity. The barriers they represent are integral to cultural life, and this is in fact what makes them attractive to people. Institutions such as a university also create barriers that need to be overcome by those committed to their intellectual development. Of course those barriers can be removed, but at the cost of losing the integrity of higher education.

Participation in the arts and education is valued because it is believed that it serves to help people engage with the institutions of society. According to one advocate of the social inclusion agenda:

> New confidence and skills; new friendships and social opportunities; cooperation towards achievement; involvement in consultation and local democracy; affirmation and questioning of identity; strengthening commitment to place; intercultural links, positive risk-taking – these ... are crucial

---

[5] Private manuscript to be published as *The Missing Plinth*.

means of fighting social exclusion. Participation in the arts does this partly by building individual and community competence, but more importantly by building belief in the possibility of positive social change.[6]

Governments throughout history have attempted to mobilize the arts to further political ends. Previously, they were used to celebrate national glory; today they are used to establish a point of contact with atomized, and often marginalized, individuals, and this strategy is deployed in a systematic and highly individualized way.

It is important to realize that the populist imperative of social engineering is neither a democratic nor an egalitarian response to the problem of social inequality or poverty. As I noted in the previous chapter, this is a project that aims to re-engage an increasingly fragmented society. Social inclusion, accessibility and participation are part of an agenda that aims to establish points of contact between the cultural elite and an otherwise estranged public. Since establishing contact constitutes the dominant objective, the question of what exactly the excluded are included *in* is seldom explored. It is easier to widen participation than to ensure that what people participate in is worthy of their involvement.

Paradoxically, policies of social engineering are generally presented as part of a programme of radical reform. This is certainly how widening participation in higher education is promoted. Yet the idea that the university is experiencing a programme of reform is a very strange one. Reforms in other spheres of life do not proceed on the assumption that the institution they are about to create will become inferior to the one that preceded it. In the postwar period, universal access to health care through the establishment of the National Health Service

6   F. Matarosso,'Use or Ornament? The Social Impact of Participation in the Art', *Comedia*, 1997.

(NHS) did not mean that the hospital was turned into a first-aid station, in the way that the university has been reinvented as a college of further education.

There is nothing new about attempting to subject culture and education to the agenda of social engineering. Critics in previous eras took issue with the celebration of art for its own sake, and disparaged the idea of the disinterested pursuit of the truth. The difference now is the way in which such attitudes are systematically conveyed and applied in all parts of social life, and the degree of reluctance to uphold any institutional values and standards at all. Accordingly today, by their very nature, institutional values and standards are obstacles to widening access, and an elitist insult to the self-esteem of the excluded.

In principle, creating equal opportunities for all is a worthwhile objective. Increasing public participation in intellectual and cultural life is a goal that anyone with democratic leanings can strongly support. It is not the case that, as conservative cultural critics have often argued, popular participation must be to the detriment of standards. The belief that 'more means worse' was, for example, the basis of Kingsley Amis' objection to the expansion of the numbers of university students in the 1960s.[7] Rather, the expansion of higher education will only lead to a fall in standards if widening participation is driven by concerns that have little to do with the promotion of the ideals of the university. It is when education and culture are dominated by concerns that are external to their agenda that more does indeed mean less.

Despite its populist rhetoric, the social exclusion agenda is deeply hostile to genuine popular culture. Genuine popular culture is self-generated rather than the product of policies that aim to engage the public. Social exclusion policies, by contrast, aim to shape public taste, standardize it and ultimately control it.

[7] Amis is cited in Shils (1972).

The attack on autonomy

As with education, cultural and arts policy has been mobilized to combat social exclusion. This instrumental deployment of cultural policy is in striking contrast to the idea that culture possesses a measure of autonomy, indeed that it should be a self-contained realm that develops in accordance with its own laws. Social engineering now shapes public policy on culture. The Department for Culture, Media and Sport seeks to make cultural resources accessible to 'the many, not just the few', and to rebrand cultural institutions as 'centres for social change'.[8] Using cultural institutions to connect the political establishment to people turns these bodies towards an objective that has little to do with their original reason for existence, and as such represents a direct challenge to their institutional independence.

Promoters of social engineering argue that institutional autonomy is no big deal since it rarely exists in practice. They sometimes contend that the quest for autonomy represents the policy of vested interests, and suggest that the idea of institutional independence, like that of knowledge for its own sake, is a sham that overlooks the fact that cultural institutions are subservient to the interests of the ruling elites. They claim that the university's traditional demand for institutional autonomy represents a claim to preserve the privileges of the already privileged. Thus, undermining the autonomy of the university is a step in the right direction, since it facilitates the project of widening access. Without diminishing its institutional independence, it is not possible to subject the university to the externally imposed demands of the social engineering agenda. That is why the access movement is so enthusiastic about getting rid of features of university life that distinguish it from other sectors of education. According to one advocate of this approach, getting rid of the

---

[8]   See DCMS (2000).

boundary that separates higher from other forms of education is necessary for encouraging greater access. Hence 'the strength, stability and clarity' of the boundaries between higher education and others 'have been questioned at different points and to various degrees by alternative access routes and relationships which anticipate new audiences and broader purposes for a "higher" education'.[9]

Breaking down 'the strength, stability and clarity' of the boundary that separates the university from the rest of society represents a self-conscious attempt to undermine the university's aspiration to institutional autonomy. In Britain, this crusade is justified on the grounds that the university serves the narrow self-interest of a powerful elite; in the US, on the grounds that the university has never been, and never will be, devoted to the pursuit of disinterested knowledge. A powerful mood of cultural cynicism drives critics to denounce the claim for autonomy. As Russell Berman, Professor in Humanities at Stanford University, wrote, today's cultural cynics 'cannot imagine a knowledge *not* complicitous with power, a science *not* dependent on the Pentagon, or teachers *not* driven solely by self-interest'.[10] Of course the critics have a point. Universities like other cultural institutions have done many things other than the disinterested pursuit of knowledge. They have on occasions served dubious economic and political agendas. However, as Berman argues, 'a critique of the universities that omits the possibility of a life of the mind is, ultimately, just anti-intellectualism'.[11]

A critique of the university that precludes the possibility of genuine search for knowledge represents an acquiescence to a

9   Gareth Parry, 'Marking and Mediating the Higher-Education Boundary', in Fulton (1989), p. 24.
10 Russell A. Berman, 'Perestroika for the University!', *Telos*, 81 (Fall 1989), p. 115.
11 Russell A. Berman, 'Perestroika for the University!', *Telos*, 81 (Fall 1989), p. 115.

perpetual climate of intellectual malaise. Yet the feeble founda-
tions for institutional independence do not constitute an
argument against trying to achieve a measure of autonomy. They
merely point to the difficulty of approximating the *ideal* of
intellectual and cultural autonomy: and the defence of such an
ideal is central to the development of a healthy society. One of the
most persuasive arguments in favour of autonomy has been
mounted by the recently deceased leftist French sociologist Pierre
Bourdieu. Bourdieu recognizes that the claim for institutional
autonomy represents a demand for a privileged status. But he
argues that 'cultural producers', as he calls them, 'can do this
without remorse or moral hesitation since, by defending
themselves as a whole they defend the universal'. Bourdieu
argues for the defence of the 'economic and social conditions
necessary for the autonomy of different fields of cultural
production', because such autonomy provides the platform from
which ideas expressing the general interests of society can be
produced.[12]

Bourdieu's strong defence of autonomy is not motivated by the
objective of distancing the university from society by turning it
into an ivory tower. Autonomy is valued because it creates a
space where cultural producers can function without being
subordinated to any external interests. However, this work is
directed towards society, and autonomy is prized because it
provides a stable foundation for the kind of cultural and
intellectual life that is worthy of society's needs.

A weaker defence of autonomy is offered by the Scottish
philosopher Gordon Graham. Graham too values academic
autonomy. But he is concerned that if it becomes an end in
itself, and if the ideas generated through it fail to have an impact
on society, then its value becomes questionable. 'Academic

---

[12] Pierre Bourdieu, 'The Corporatism of the Universal: The Role of
Intellectuals in the Modern World', *Telos* 81 (Fall 1989), p. 103.

autonomy, which crucially includes freedom of thought and inquiry, is rendered much less valuable than it might be if the thinking it protects has little or no influence on the general formation of social ideas', he writes.[13] Graham is of course right that society will not protect that which it does not value. As both Bourdieu and Graham recognize, in the end intellectuals and artists have to create ideas and objects of value for a wider society. But they do not create it on demand or in response to external pressure, but through the inner dynamic and the external interaction of specific cultural fields.

Despite the prevailing mood of philistinism, proponents of the social engineering agenda are from time to time still forced to pay lip-service to the ideal of valuing culture for its own sake. 'We should not lose sight of the fact that participation in sporting and cultural activities are an end in themselves and enrich people's lives every single day', states the DCMS 2003 Annual Plan. However, such statements are swiftly subordinated to a more instrumentalist approach towards the arts. It appears that the arts are important for 'improving [educational] attainment and behaviour, and encouraging lifelong learning; helping to combat crime and create safe, active and cohesive communities, [and] . . . making a very substantial contribution to the economy'.[14] Such instrumentalist appreciation of the arts introduces criteria for assessing it that has nothing to do with its own qualities. Through focusing on the impact of art on a variety of social issues, it ceases to be judged according to standards internal to art, and thereby loses its ability to determine its own direction.

Bourdieu believed that one of the main sites of struggle for intellectuals is over the question of how the worth of their work is

---

[13] Graham (2002), p. 122.

[14] Cited by Adrian Ellis, 'Valuing Culture; A Background Note', paper for 'Agenda for Valuing Culture', conference organized by DEMOS, London, 17 June 2003.

assessed. He warned that the 'most serious danger, however, is the tendency to strip intellectuals of their prerogatives to evaluate themselves and their production according to their own criteria'.[15] Once the value of cultural and intellectual work is determined by institutions external to the domain of cultural production, it becomes subject to influences that encourage conformism and bureaucratization. One symptom of this regrettable turn of events is that culture and education are increasingly quantified and measured, rather than valued.

Traditionally, artists and intellectuals have been sensitive to the demands placed on their activities through commercial pressures. In response, they have attempted to insulate their activities from these pressures in order to retain a measure of control over their work. Unfortunately, this self-conscious reaction is relatively feeble in response to political pressures, and there has been little opposition mounted by today's intellectuals and artists to prevent the introduction of bureaucratic or market-driven evaluation of their work. As a result, evaluation in accordance with criteria that is external to intellectual and cultural endeavour has proceeded with alarming speed. Directors of museums and art galleries have tended to roll over and accept the attempts of policy-makers to evaluate cultural institutions in accordance with an agenda that has nothing to do with intellectual or artistic development. One example of this instrumental approach towards culture is a recently announced scheme involving the arts and a community organization in Cleveland, Ohio, which aims to discover whether the arts can help children avoid drugs and risky behaviour. The local arts group has been assigned the task of creating an arts curriculum for 300 African-American youth ages 11–14 to see whether involvement in the arts 'helps participants increase their

---

[15] Pierre Bourdieu, 'The Corporatism of the Universal: The Role of Intellectuals in the Modern World', *Telos* 81 (Fall 1989), p. 106.

self-esteem, self-expression and other attributes that help prevent HIV and AIDS infection'.[16]

In the US, the arts are also promoted on the grounds that they help heal conflict and bring the community together. 'It's becoming more evident than ever that culture not only nourishes but heals, and that it is a significant stabilizing force for a society under duress', observed one art critic in the aftermath of 9/11. He added: 'as maintaining the viability of American steel mills is necessary for defence, keeping our cultural base vital is essential for the country's spirit'. The idea that art serves a therapeutic role is frequently communicated by members of the cultural establishment. After 9/11, Philippe de Montebello, director of New York's Metropolitan Museum, compared his institution with that of a hospital. Hospitals are there to 'fix the body', he remarked: 'we're here to fix the soul'.[17]

There has been little objection from artists and cultural workers to British Government ministers' claims that the arts are 'good for your health'; that 'the arts have a key role in making our society a better place to live'; or that the arts 'can help tackle crime'.[18] The Arts Council and local cultural services have swiftly internalized the agenda of social inclusion. Thus the director of Leisure and Cultural Services at Wigan Council promotes the benefits of sports, art and play on the grounds that these activities 'improve cognitive and social skills; reduce impulsiveness and risk-taking behaviours; raise self-esteem and self-confidence and improve education and employment prospects'.[19] The government has established a special team of advisors called a PAT

[16] *The Plain Dealer*, 23 October 2003.
[17] Cited in Mary Thomas, 'For a shared expression of emotions, we turn to the arts', *Pittsburgh Post-Gazette*, 11 November 2001.
[18] Cited in Sara Selwood 'Measuring Culture', *Spiked-online*, 30 December 2002.
[19] See 'Realising the potential for cultural services', Wigan Council, 17 December 2001.

(Policy Action Team), which specializes in policies that target social exclusion through raising the self-esteem of the excluded. The Policy Action Team 10 social inclusion report to the DCMS acknowledged the potential problems with subordinating cultural services to demands of therapeutic recognition. 'We do not believe that every artist or sportsperson should be a social worker by another name, or that artistic or sporting excellence should take second place to community regeneration', it noted.[20] However, artistic excellence was conspicuously absent from the examples of best practice that the report promoted. One scheme praised by PAT 10 was a centre in Manchester, where people recovering from mental illness 'find that the arts are not merely a powerful antidote to loneliness, but also a significant means of self-fulfilment and of giving pleasure to others'.[21] This goal of transforming Britain's cultural institutions into centres for therapeutic engagement with excluded people is one of the clearest illustrations of the project to reorient them towards the demands of social policy. The lack of public opposition to this policy also indicates that many people working in this sector have little problem with becoming absorbed into the new cultural bureaucracy.

To ensure that these objectives are achieved, the DCMS is keenly interested in evaluating the impact that its policies are having. As the cultural theorist Sara Selwood, argues: 'the gathering of evidence about the impact of the arts has assumed centre-stage in cultural policy'.[22] In a similar vein, the university has become one of the most intensely audited institutions in society. Every aspect of university life, from teaching, to student progression, to modes of assessment and research, are now systematically audited. One of the direct consequences of this

[20] *Building on PAT 10 – Progress Report on Social Inclusion,* February 2001, p. 5.
[21] ibid., p. 22.
[22] Sara Selwood, 'Measuring Culture', *Spiked-online*, 30 December 2002.

process is the erosion of the autonomy of the university. Academics are now expected to work according to criteria established by the external auditor, civil servant and politicians. Auditing does not merely measure: it alters and ultimately transforms how a university works. This development is described by Shore and Wright in the following terms:

> Audit heralded a significant break with the principle of academic autonomy. Rather than attacking university autonomy head on, the government concealed the extent of its intervention by recruiting a host of intermediary agencies and by mobilizing academics themselves as managerial professionals and active accomplices in this process.[23]

Auditing leads to the colonization of higher education by the educational bureaucracy. Colonization works best through collaborators and the system of auditing is directed to the task of creating a coterie of experts who police the auditing process. As Shore and Wright note: 'central to the development of new political technologies in higher education has been the creation of new categories of experts including "educational development consultants", "quality assurance officers", "staff development trainers" and "teaching quality assessors"'.[24]

The new group of auditors inside cultural and educational institutions play an active role in weakening the integrity of the intellectual activity pursued. As Pierre Bourdieu noted, their loyalty is not to the institution but to the external system of auditing: 'Thanks to their activities, extraneous norms replace those particular to a given field of cultural production'.[25] The

---

[23] See Chris Shore and Susan Wright, 'Coercive accountability; the rise of audit culture in higher education', in Strahern (2000), p. 68.

[24] See Chris Shore and Susan Wright, 'Coercive accountability; the rise of audit culture in higher education', in Strahern (2000), p. 62.

[25] Pierre Bourdieu, 'The Corporatism of the Universal: The Role of Intellectuals in the Modern World', *Telos* 81 (Fall 1989), p. 105.

auditing ethos forces individuals to submit to a regime that seeks to quantify and inspect their efforts, promoting bite-sized, easily standardized effort that can be easily measured, weighed and served to an infantilized public.

Social engineering and the market

What is the worst insult that can be directed at a university? Probably that it is an elitist ivory tower, out of touch with the real world. Yet there was a time when the opposite accusation was more hurtful. Thirty years ago, the radical historian E. P. Thompson could think of no better way of condemning his institution than to label it Warwick University Ltd. The things that Thompson disliked about Warwick – its corporate structure, its cosy relationship to business, and its obsession with training students for the job market – are today seen as entirely desirable. The modern university does not remain proudly aloof from the business world, but gets stuck into licensing new inventions, consulting with corporations and spinning out high-tech companies.

Traditionally the power of the market has been seen as the main threat to academic autonomy and artistic integrity. The tension between the world of the intellectual and that of business has been widely commented on. For example, the dissidence of intellectuals is explained by the French political theorist Bertrand de Jouvenal as a consequence of an inevitable conflict between the values of the business classes and creative artists. Business is institutionally committed to giving its clientele what they want. By contrast, the creative artist views the worth of his products independently of their market value. As de Jouvenal states: 'the businessman offers to the public "goods" defined as anything the public will buy; the intellectual seeks to teach what is "good", and to him some of the goods offered are things of no value which the public should be discouraged from wanting'.[26]

Historical studies of the university recognize that there has often been a conflict between the values of business and trade, and the pursuit of academic work. From the standpoint of business, the customer is always right. It is not the job of a trader to question or criticize the tastes and values of potential customers. Academics, however, are frequently educating their students' tastes and encouraging them to question their values. Indeed one of the most distinct and important features of academic and intellectual activity is precisely that which cannot be dominated by an instrumental ethos. Academic pedagogy – unlike the service provided by a language school – does not seek to offer what the customer wants, but attempts to provide what the student needs. Artists who produce great art do not ask the question 'what does the public want?' They seek to express something through their art, rather than merely produce an object for sale.

The tension between the values of the business classes and creative artists has made many intellectuals weary of the influence of the market. Commercial and business pressure has always been seen as a potential threat to the exercise of academic and artistic integrity. The market is indifferent to the intrinsic merit of a cultural product – it is interested only in its monetary worth. Commercial considerations create strong pressures towards the popularization of art forms and ideas. That is why advocates of social inclusion often attempt to harness market forces to drive forward their own project – through emptying educational and cultural institutions of any intrinsic worth, market forces can direct them towards objectives set externally by the social engineering agenda.

The capacity of the market to erode the autonomy and

[26] Cited in De G. B. Huszar (1960), p. 395.

integrity of the university was noted by Peter Scott, the former editor of *The Times Higher Education Supplement,* when he contrasted previous attitudes towards the university with those that prevailed in the 1990s:

> Then higher education was seen as something to be deserved, to be aspired to; now it is increasingly regarded as something to be purchased by the prudent or fortunate. There is now a powerful movement away from the idea of higher education as a public service. It is no longer to be seen as a cultural, even moral, enterprise in which the notion of intellectual authority plays a key role, but as an economic enterprise in which customers, whether students or others, are enabled to buy services.[27]

This shift of focus may indeed help to reduce the obstacles to wider access. For if higher education is stripped of its deeper cultural significance and is regarded in more commonplace instrumental terms, there is less need to regulate access to the system. This point is clearly understood by sections of the access movement who regard market forces as a useful counterweight against institutional autonomy. The mass market is seen as an ally that would force the university to yield to the demands of populist social engineering.[28]

The convergence between the ethos of consumerism and the agenda of inclusion has helped forge a formidable power that continually impacts on institutions of culture and education. This synthesis of consumerism and populism provides legitimation for the social engineering agenda. Consumer choice and individual access merge into a populist ethos that regards culture and education as consisting of bite-size commodities that can be spoon-fed to Joe Public.

---

[27] Peter Scott, 'Post-binary access and learning', in Parry and Wake (1990), pp. 30–1.

[28] This argument is advanced in Peter Wright, 'Putting learning at the Centre of Higher Education', in Fulton (1989).

Although advocates of the marketization of culture tend to be suspicious of government-led policies of social engineering, they too regard the erosion of cultural and academic autonomy as, on balance, a positive development. From their standpoint, the assimilation of cultural institutions into the market has led to an artistic and intellectual renaissance. Like the proponents of the inclusion agenda, the advocates of the marketization of culture reject the idea that we are going through a period of philistinism. Rather than dumbing down, they claim that society is wising up. This thesis is argued with force by Tyler Cowen, who in his book *In Praise of Commercial Culture* claims that the free market does the best job of promoting cultural excellence. As a result of the workings of the capitalist market, he argues, the United States is going through a cultural renaissance able to provide a 'parade of successful and diverse cultural products'.[29]

Market advocates such as Cowen sustain their thesis by pointing to the quantitative expansion of cultural life in the US. One of his supporters argues that 'during the past *few decades, we have been experiencing what can aptly be* called a "cultural boom": a massive increase in art, music, literature, video, and other forms of creative expression'.[30] This increase in the consumption of cultural goods, which is linked to the growth of prosperity, is seen as evidence of the contemporary boom of culture. There is little doubt that the consumption of culture had become a dynamic feature of contemporary society – however, evidence of increasing cultural consumption tells us little about the quality of what is being consumed. This focus on consumption confuses the public's aspiration for entertainment and distraction with the development of ideas and art. As Hannah Arendt noted back in the sixties, what we have is not mass culture

---

[29] Cowen (2000).
[30] Nick Gillespie, 'All Culture, All the Time', in *Reason*, April 1999.

'but mass entertainment, feeding on the cultural objects of the world'.[31]

Arendt took the view that the marketization of cultural products leads to their degradation, warning that 'culture is being destroyed in order to yield entertainment'. She added:

> The result of this is not disintegration but decay, and those who promote it are not the Tin Pan Alley composers but a special kind of intellectual, often well read and well informed, whose sole function is to organize, disseminate, and change cultural objects in order to persuade the masses that *Hamlet* can be as entertaining as *My Fair Lady*, and perhaps as educational as well. There are many great authors of the past who have survived centuries of oblivion and neglect, but it is still an open question whether they will be able to survive an entertaining version of what they have to say.[32]

Arendt's warnings about the 'special kind of intellectual' who peddles *Hamlet* as a product of entertainment have proved to be prescient. The instrumental orientation towards art and education dominates contemporary cultural life. The main problem today, however, is not the expansion of the entertainment industry, but the crusade to spoon-feed culture to the public led by the social inclusion agenda.

Although Arendt's misgivings about the capture of culture by the entertainment industry need to be taken seriously, her pessimism cannot account for the flourishing of intellectual and artistic life alongside and in interaction with mass entertainment. Cultural life exists in a relation of uneasy tension with the market and, despite the pressure of commerce, intellectuals and artists have been able to create and develop ideas. There is little doubt that today, as in the past, the commercial imperative works

---

[31] Arendt (1993); originally written as 'The Crisis in Culture' in 1961.
[32] Arendt (1993), 'The Crisis in Culture'.

towards commodifying knowledge and art. Nevertheless, the market also provides opportunities for creativity and can provide space, albeit limited, for the pursuit of excellence. The problem today is not the growth of stupefying entertainment but the lack of affirmation for the promotion of intellectual and artistic standards. Commerce does not have a view on what kind of exhibit a museum should show, or whether university students should or should not write essays. The social inclusion agenda, however, is prepared to use both political influence and market forces to achieve its objective. The imperative of social engineering, rather than the market, today represents the greatest threat to the integrity of intellectual and cultural production. Compared to the politics of inclusion, the problems posed by the entertainment industry pale into insignificance.

5   The Culture of Flattery

There is now a barely contested consensus within the cultural and education establishment that access and social inclusion should be at the heart of the missions of cultural institutions. At conferences, officials and administrators routinely demand that universities, libraries, museums and galleries should place inclusion at the centre of their activities. Those seeking a career in the educational or cultural industry frequently boast that they have succeeded in transforming their institution into one that has eliminated all barriers to participation. The barriers they have in mind are not only physical obstacles to disabled access, or monetary costs that may deter the poor from paying for the price of entry, but the intellectual challenge facing people participating in educational and cultural activities. 'Once they were called museums,' notes a review of interactivity in museums in San Francisco. 'Now they're more like amusement parks.'[1]

In Britain, there is a systematic attempt to reorient the cultural institutes from dealing with serious subjects to mounting exhibitions that are directly accessible to people. 'For a variety of reasons people think galleries are too imposing, or that art has little or no relevance to their lives, is elitist, or simply boring', observes a report by the Tyne and Wear Museum. The solution proposed by this Museum is to provide the public with what the cultural elite believes people can handle. It has adopted access

---

[1]   See Steven Winn, 'Interactive Museums', *San Francisco Chronicle*, 19 July 2003.

policies that have 'encouraged the display of works from the collections which may not necessarily be famous or highly regarded, but have been chosen by members of the public simply because they like them or because they arouse certain emotions or memories'.[2] This approach is vigorously pursued by the DCMS, and all the projects it funds now have to publish access targets and detail measures by which they are 'widening access to a broad cross-section of the public for example by age, social class, and ethnicity'.[3] Not surprisingly institutions are attempting to meet access targets by any means that work. Cafés, meeting places, computer facilities and interactive entertainment are considered legitimate activities to get more people to walk through the doors. 'An ace caff with quite a nice museum attached' was the slogan of Saatchi and Saatchi's ad campaign for the V&A. This sums up the attitude of the cultural establishment towards its own institutions. It is now never clear whether museums are masquerading as drop-in centres, or community centres pretending to be museums

Whereas the cultural establishment is intensely proud of its accomplishment of turning museums into community memorials or interactive amusement parks, those who run higher education are still slightly abashed about advertising the fact that they are in the business of transforming universities into high schools. University students are increasingly treated as customers leading to what the American sociologist George Ritzer has called the McDonaldization of the university. As consumers, students are implicitly encouraged to adopt the passive attitude of receiving a service, rather than actively participating in their studies. As a result the conceptual difference between studying in a university and being taught in a school has become blurred. As Gordon

---

[2] See www.culture.gov.uk/pdf/musums.pdf + %22museums + for + the + many %22&hl = en&ieUTF-8.

[3] *Museums for the Many*, DCMS, 1999

Graham notes there is a qualitative difference between these activities: 'while *pupils* are for the most part directed by others, *students* are expected to be much more self-directed'.[4] Sadly, in many institutions, university teaching rarely promotes the kind of self-directed studying that involves the journey of discovery.

In the United States, the McDonaldization of the university has evolved in a haphazard manner in response to market pressure. In the UK this development has been more systematically implemented through a centralized higher education system. Auditing agencies like the Institute for Learning and Teaching in Higher Education have fostered a climate in which teaching has become standardized, and reduced to the role of providing students with easily digestible spoonfuls of information. This process is most clearly symbolized by the ascendancy of the 'handout culture'. Lecture notes transmitted through the web, and numerous other teaching aids, form the staple diet of many university students' learning experience. This so-called inclusive pedagogy is sometimes rationalized on the ground that it helps students overcome unnecessary barriers such as reading serious scholarly monographs. Such dumbed-down practices are presented as part of a new student-centred curriculum.

Flattering students is fast becoming an important institutional norm. Students are frequently not expected to study but to learn. Because complex ideas are not in fact learned, but studied, the intellectual horizon of the learner is restricted to the assimilation of information and the acquisition of skills. In principle, every teaching technique is worth a try. But the manner in which the ILT promotes its student-centred techniques indicates that its main objective is to keep students engaged and happy. For example, group work is used in a way similar to 'circle-time' in primary education. While this technique may make sense when used with five-year-olds, in the university it serves to distract

4   Graham (2002), p. 36.

students from gaining knowledge through intellectual struggle and hard work. In effect the inclusive agenda infantilizes university students. The role of academics, meanwhile, is to 'support' rather than transform undergraduates. Academics are discouraged from acting as teachers: they, too, are labelled learners on new 'student-centred' campuses.

Widening access to education is not a novel idea. Social reformers in the Victorian era, for example John Ruskin, argued that the working classes should be included in education so that all could appreciate the wonders of human intellectual endeavour. What is distinct about the access movement today is that it is entirely focused on the opening up of educational opportunities while being quite indifferent to the intellectual content of the experience. The access movement makes no pretence of aspiring to an intellectual ideal. Its pedagogy self-consciously eschews cultivating people's appreciation of humanity's cultural achievements, by emphasizing inclusion rather than education, and striving to appeal to the lowest common denominator of the public's imagination. The access movement is profoundly hostile to pedagogic practices, standards and expectations that distinguish the university from other types of educational institutions. Research presented to the European Access Network in July 2001 criticized the 'enormous differences between the approaches and cultures of community education, further education and higher education'.[5] The project of re-launching the university as a community college of further education represents the height of ambition of the access movement.

The aspiration of inclusion is not a new focus for policy-making. Previous political regimes sought to use the institutions of culture and education to integrate different sections of society into a symbolic community. However, such policies were justified

---

[5]   Cited in Claire Fox, 'The Massification of Higher Education', in Hayes and Wynyard (2002), p. 139.

on the grounds that they helped raise the level of public culture. For example, the nineteenth century British elite sought to give institutional expression to high aesthetic standards in order to assist the task of social integration. 'The highest instruments of human cultivation are also ultimate guarantees of public order', stated Gladstone.[6] Gladstone and his associates took the view that refining public taste would lead to moral improvement, which in turn would assist the integration of the unpredictable masses into the social order. However manipulative and instrumental their motivation, at least the public gained access to some decent museums and art galleries as a result. Today, the policy of inclusion makes no attempt to cultivate and elevate the public taste. On the contrary, it regards the taste of the public as something to flatter and institutionalize. In place of social integration it makes do with providing interactive entertainment for an otherwise disengaged public. 'In the past, people tended to view museums as equivalent to schools', decries Maeryta Medrano, co-founder of Gyroscope Inc., an Oakland-based company that designs interactive exhibits for museums around the US. Medrano is in the business of making sure that museums become Disneyfied, and seems delighted that more and more museums 'have become places where people have a kind of shared social experience'.[7] 'A kind of shared social experience' turns out to be a roundabout way of saying that customers of the Disneyfied museum share the experience of interacting with the gadgets favoured by today's cultural entrepreneurs.

The cultural politics of the nineteenth century are today often castigated as paternalistic and elitist. In this vein, British historian Stefan Collini states that 'this model had its paternalist side – the mandarins knew what was worth having more of whether people

[6]   Cited in Minihan (2001), p. 36.
[7]   Cited in Steven Winn, 'Interactive Museums', *San Francisco Chronicle*, 19 July 2003.

clamoured for it or not'.[8] There is little doubt it was not popular demand, but the belief that certain forms of culture could uplift public taste, which motivated Gladstone and his colleagues. Theirs was very much a top-down policy of cultivating public attitudes consistent with the prevailing cultural norms of the Victorian elite. However, it is necessary to note that today's social inclusion policy is no more democratic than its nineteenth-century counterpart. Social inclusion is not a response to popular demand. There are no masses of people demonstrating to be included in the museums, universities and art galleries that have adopted the agenda of social inclusion. The very language in which inclusion policies are framed – 'learning outcomes', 'lifelong learning', 'reinforcing self-esteem' – is one that most people would find incomprehensible. These are words invented by cultural mandarins for use in their bureaucratic world. Many of the recently created cultural institutions that have been launched as self-consciously populist initiatives have failed to attract public support. The Millennium Dome indicates that it takes more than the institutionalization of inclusiveness to attract people's interest. The technologically sophisticated, but dumbed-down, exhibitions at Bradford Cathedral have proved to be a flop, as has an expensively built museum devoted to the celebration of popular music in Sheffield.

'Why do we continue to build certain cultural institutions such as museums at an accelerating rate?' is the question posed by two proponents of the cultural inclusion agenda.[9] There is a variety of motifs for the growth of the museum industry – urban regeneration, the promotion of tourism, the imperative of creating new symbols of community and the dictates of social engineering. But whatever drives the growth of this sector, it is certainly not popular demand. Indeed many of these projects

---

8   See Stefan Collini, 'HiEdBiz', *London Review of Books*, 6 November 2003.
9   See Pachter and Landry (2001), p. 37.

justify their existence on the grounds that they can create a demand for inclusion. Often policies of inclusion are oriented towards creating incentives for people who are indifferent to what's on offer to sign up to the inclusion agenda. This process of attempting to create a demand for inclusion is particularly striking in higher education. There, officials openly write about creating an aspiration to participate in higher education among those who lack such an ambition. In June 2001, a statement on widening participation issued by Universities UK observed that 'the key issue for the sector now is attracting people with no background of (or current aspirations to) study in HE to courses and universities'. In other words, widening participation has little to do with meeting a real demand for a place in a university. It means getting people to come to university regardless of whether or not they have such aspirations.

Inclusion is a policy peddled by bureaucrats for reasons that have little to do with culture or education. Its approach is no less top-down than that of its nineteenth-century predecessors. The policy is driven by officials who think they know best what the public needs, while pretending to be responding to public opinion. But what distinguishes this approach is its total disregard for both public demand and for concerns that are genuinely cultural or educational in character. At least Gladstone and his colleagues sometimes sought to cultivate and inspire the public imagination. The one-dimensional approach of the inclusion agenda is simply to flatter it.

Inclusion through affirmation

Social inclusion is one of those fashionable concepts like transparency and accountability, which everyone uses but rarely defines. Virtually every policy claims to be inclusive, and it is rare to hear any figure of authority attack attempts to institutionalize social inclusion. As a result, social inclusion is generally accorded the status of a public virtue. As noted previously, policies of inclusion are underwritten by the political elite's desire to establish or re-establish a point of contact with an otherwise atomized and disengaged public. There is nothing objectionable or unworthy about this motive. The problem is that this policy rarely directs attention to the fundamental social, economic and cultural causes of people's estrangement from many of the key institutions of society. Instead, inclusion is represented primarily as a psychological process of validating people in order to make them feel good. The corollary of this principle is that public bodies, including cultural and educational ones, should do everything possible to avoid undertaking initiatives that may make people feel bad or not even good about themselves. As a result, schools must ensure that their pupils never experience failure or lack affirmation, and that they possess high levels of self-esteem. University lecturers are put under pressure to mark positively, and to provide a climate of support where no undergraduate feels intimidated or offended. Galleries and museums are charged with affirming visitors, and ensuring that they don't feel overwhelmed or daunted by their experience.

In June 2003, Professor Christopher Smout complained about the dumbing down of the National Museums of Scotland. His comment followed a policy statement from six museums, which put historical research at the end of a list of eleven priorities. The response of Gordon Rintoul, Director of the National Museum of Scotland, summed up the approach of the tuned-in cultural mandarin, by indicating that his mission was to expand the museum's learning and events programmes for the public to ensure that 'we fulfil our educational role and provide enjoyment for our visitors'.[10] So the official policy of affirmation is: No to research, yes to fun.

---

[10] Cited in the *Daily Telegraph*, 21 July 2003.

The therapeutics of affirmation that drive the social inclusion agenda is spelled out by Tyne and Wear museums in the following terms:

Since 1993 several Tyne and Wear museums and galleries have shown community exhibitions chosen and curated by local people. Five main aims underpin these projects: to give people greater confidence in their own ability to assess and to appreciate art, to provide wider access to the gallery collection and a better understanding of how a gallery works, to make visitors aware that art can be interpreted in a variety of different ways and that there is no one right answer, to create an enjoyable and stimulating experience for both participants and gallery visitors, and to focus particularly on people with disabilities and disadvantaged groups as a way of encouraging confidence and self-esteem.[11]

On both sides of the Atlantic, the mission statements of cultural and educational institutions are peppered with references to undertaking the task of encouraging confidence and self-esteem. Unfortunately, the worthy objective of making people feel good about themselves is not always consistent with the genuine demands made on a person by authentic cultural and educational experiences. Trying to make sense of complex ideas and art forms can be at times a dispiriting experience. Such experience necessarily involves the act of discovery – which can be intimidating, frightening and confusing. No wonder that so often we feel very small, disoriented and defensive when confronted with challenging experiences. And often when we do poorly, it is difficult not to feel bad about ourselves.

It is precisely because an intellectual journey involves unexpected tests and challenges that it is ill-suited to the task

[11] See www.culture.gov.uk/pdf/musums.pdf + %22museums + for + the + many %22&hl = en&ieUTF-8.

of providing unquestioned affirmation. That is why the cultural and educational experience dictated by the agenda of social inclusion has little to do with a journey of discovery – and why institutions committed to the policy of social inclusion end up *excluding* challenging experiences from their premises. This process is particularly striking in primary education. Instead of attempting to inspire children through challenging and stretching them, the education system is devoted to making them feel good. The premise of current pedagogy is that children, particularly those who are disadvantaged, need constant affirmation if they are to succeed. 'At some point in the last few decades, the educational world came to agree that its overriding priority was to make children feel good about themselves: none should feel inferior to anyone else or a failure', notes Melanie Phillips.[12] As Phillips notes, ensuring that children possess high self-esteem has become a fundamental premise of the inclusivist agenda.

Concern with raising or maintaining children's self-esteem is based on the assumption that children are far too fragile to deal with being tested and challenged. It is frequently suggested that they need to be insulated from the experience of failure if they are to avoid permanent emotional damage. Inclusion and affirmation are therefore fundamentally at odds with a challenging curriculum that stretches children in order to realize their potential. The education system has become dominated by what US critic Maureen Stout has called The Feel-Good Curriculum, which means that 'teachers lower their expectation of students, which research shows is one of the most damaging things we can do, since students will fulfil our expectations, high or low'.[13]

A preoccupation with children's self-esteem has fostered a preoccupation towards attending to children's emotional needs – often at the expense of intellectual ones. The school is gradually

---

[12] Phillips (1998), p. 12.
[13] Stout (2000), p. 160.

becoming transformed into a clinic. Is it any surprise that the UK-based Mental Health Foundation has recommended that schools should constitute a focal point for mental health intervention? Leading educationalists argue that schools spend too much time promoting intellectual subjects and too little on social and emotional skills. The UK government's advisory group on education for citizenship and the teaching of democracy in schools considers self-esteem an important core skill. The Department for Education's guiding statement on 'sex and relationship' education instructs schools to build pupils' self-esteem. The growing influence of the 'feel-good curriculum' indicates that children's education is increasingly subject to the dictates of the agenda of affirmation through inclusion.

The attempt to insulate children from challenging and painful experiences is often motivated by an understandable desire to protect them from the harsh realities of life. Unfortunately this sentiment has been transformed into an ideology that dictates that those children's feelings must be protected at all costs. As the objective of protecting children's feelings becomes an end in itself, so the pedagogy of praise and affirmation has encouraged intellectual complacency in the schools. There is a systematic attempt to abolish the perception of failure, and children can expect continuous praise and gold stars for their effort. The implicit message transmitted to pupils is that you are judged on effort, rather than what you have achieved. As Stout notes, 'this idea destroys the notion of working toward a goal and thereby undermines the very idea of excellence'.[14]

The reluctance to make value judgements about what children have achieved has been extended to the world of adulthood. There, too, the desire to protect people's feelings is 'judged more important than the desire to stimulate real creativity or instil respect for special achievement'. As John Tusa notes in his essay

[14] Stout (2000), p. 163.

'On Creativity', 'in the process of valuing every individual's worth and effort, the definition of creativity was extended so widely that it almost undermined any belief in its true meaning: the exceptional act of imaginative discovery and expression in an art form'.[15] Consequently, the agenda of inclusion through affirmation has a negative impact, not only on children's education, but on intellectual and cultural life in general.

The institutionalization of recognition

The agenda of social inclusion represents an attempt to give meaning to people's lives through providing individuals with a sense of affirmation. It aims to respond to circumstances in which people have lost the web of meaning that would once have enabled them to understand who they are and where they stand in relation to others. However, social inclusion avoids the question of how *communities* can forge a web of meaning through which people can make sense of their lives and ensure that their actions are affirmed. Instead, inclusion is oriented towards the atomized individual, and leaves the big questions in abeyance.

Today's society appears to possess a diminished capacity to answer the question of who we are. One symptom of this trend is the politicization of identities. As the American social commentator Jedediah Purdy has remarked, 'identity politics, based on sex, sexuality, and, mostly, race and ethnicity, suggests that politics should work not so much to give people *things* such as education and jobs as to give them *recognition*'.[16] The growth of identity politics and the consequent demand for recognition has had a significant influence on contemporary political discourse and policy making. The policy of social inclusion

---

[15] John Tusa, 'On Creativity', in Tusa (2003), p. 6.
[16] Purdy (1999), p. 64.

represents an attempt to respond to this demand, and to cultivate it further.

The reorientation of government towards the project of affirming people is linked to the objective of forging a stable relationship with people in society. This development represents an attempt to confront the problem of legitimation faced by authorities throughout the Western world.[17] Recognition through the institution of the state involves a mix of policies that seek to affirm and validate the individual, and attempting to make people feel good about themselves is a central motif of this process. Therapeutic techniques are employed throughout the public sphere: since the early 1980s, when counselling emerged as a government policy directed at reintegrating the unemployed, therapeutic intervention has become a normal feature of social policy.[18] Moreover, the loss of credibility in the project of classical welfarism has encouraged the state to adopt a more individualized and therapeutic style of policy making. In both the UK and the US, policies are increasingly represented as 'supporting' and 'empowering', if not quite treating, individuals.

Policies developed since the mid-1990s do not aim to 'solve' problems so much as to support otherwise disempowered clients and target groups. This is particularly the case with policies that are designed to tackle social exclusion. The manner in which the language of social exclusion and inclusion is used conveys the impression that people suffer from disadvantage as a psychological condition of their existence. Disadvantage is frequently depicted as the consequence of the absence of affirmation: a state of mind caused by the absence of self-worth. Norman Fairclough's study of the language of New Labour suggests that social exclusion is conceptualized as a 'condition people are in, not something that is done to them. Social exclusion is rarely

---

[17] This point is further explored in Furedi (2003).
[18] See Furedi (2003), chapter 4.

presented as a process but rather something like illness that people suffer from.'[19] It is not so much about poverty or economic disadvantage, but the feeling of not being a part of the important institutions of society. The premise upon which this version of the problem is based is that people become excluded because they lack the sense of self-worth to participate in the institutions of society. That is why institutions need to affirm such individuals if they are to break down the apparent barriers to inclusion.

The experience of social exclusion is frequently presented as a subjective one. 'Social exclusion is perceived and experienced "subjectively"', write the authors of a 1999 report for the Scottish Executive. This report presents social exclusion as a form of social isolation that encompasses 'lack of contact with other people, a feeling of being trapped, low self-esteem and self-confidence, and feelings of insecurity, hopelessness and depression'.[20] The Library and Information Commission's report *Libraries: the essence of inclusion* echoes the same point, indicating that social exclusion is experienced subjectively and is therefore 'specific and relative to each individual, group or environment'.[21] Here the erosion of civic solidarity and informal networks is recast as essentially a psychological problem, to which education and culture are offered as an antidote. The policy of lifelong learning is frequently justified on the grounds that it helps to raise the self-esteem of communities and individuals. As Kathryn Ecclestone notes in her study of lifelong learning: 'ideas about creating "safe spaces", "privileging the learner's voice", and offering people recognition and "positive

---

[19] N. Fairclough, (2000), *New Labour, New Language?*, London: Routledge, pp. 54–5.

[20] William O'Connor and Jane Lewis, 'Experiences of Social Exclusion in Scotland', Scottish Executive. Central Research Unit, Research Programme Research Findings No. 73, 1999.

[21] Library and Information Commission, *Libraries: the essence of inclusion*, 2000.

unconditional regard" ' influence the discussion on this subject. They have led to a focus on 'the psychological and emotional minutiae of people's "fragile learning identities", learning biographies and narratives'.[22] This emphasis on conferring affirmation and recognition tends to subordinate the experience of education to that of treatment – in this case, for life.

The psychological dimension is decisive in the representation of exclusion. The Library and Information Commission explicitly focuses on what it calls the 'psychology of exclusion', noting that 'individuals may become excluded through experiencing or perceiving alienation; isolation; lack of identity; low self-confidence, low self-esteem; passivity; dependence, bewilderment, fear, anger, apathy, low aspirations and hopelessness'.[23] Tackling this psychology of exclusion is not justified simply on the grounds that it assists social integration, but also because managing this condition of psychological distress is interpreted as an integral part of the business of the cultural and educational establishment. Thus inclusion, both at the level of policy making and that of culture, represents an attempt to fulfil the demand for recognition and affirmation

In its most extreme form, the ethos of inclusion subordinates social and cultural policies to the exigencies of recognition and the therapeutic ethos. In the domain of culture, the Department for Culture, Media and Sport (DCMS) has vigorously promoted the inclusion agenda through projects that make people feel good about themselves. It has targeted museums, galleries, cultural organizations like the Arts Council, and local cultural services, to adopt its therapeutic approach. A document published by the DCMS, *Centres for Social Change: Museums, Galleries and Archives for All,* demands that curators of museums and galleries

---

[22] Kathryn Ecclestone, 'Lifelong learning: education or therapy?', *Spiked-online,* 28 January 2003.
[23] Kathryn Ecclestone, 'Lifelong learning: education or therapy?', *Spiked-online,* 28 January 2003.

take on board the objective of 'combating social exclusion', and instructs curators that they have a duty to 'increase individuals' self-worth, value and motivation' and to raise 'self-esteem'.[24] The goal of transforming Britain's cultural institutions into centres for therapeutic engagement with excluded people is one of the clearest illustrations of the project to construct a public infrastructure for the cultivation of a therapeutic ethos. This project represents the most distinctive feature of cultural policy today.

Although the concept of social inclusion is vague, and used to refer to a wide variety of problems, its central focus is to establish a series of linkages between formal institutions and the excluded. Policy statements across government departments continually adopt the rhetoric, and in recent years there has been a systematic attempt to present policies in the sphere of sports, culture and arts from the perspective of inclusion.[25] The Northern Ireland Executive has also adopted this approach. One of its recent consultation papers affirmed the need to help 'increase social inclusion and build self-esteem through participation in culture, arts and leisure activities'.[26]

Government policy and elite interests have always influenced the direction adopted by cultural and educational institutions. However, with the exception of totalitarian regimes, most governments have tended at least to pay lip-service to valuing education and the arts for their own sake. Today, the imperative of social engineering overwhelms such sentiments. Even experts involved in the field of cultural policy have adopted the language of the social engineer, and are likely to adopt arguments such as this:

New confidence and skills; new friendships and social

[24] Department of Culture, Media and Sports, *Centres for Social Change: Museums, Galleries and Archives for All.*
[25] Sports Scotland (2000), *Social Inclusion.*
[26] Northern Ireland Executive (2000), *Investing for Health*, Belfast, p. 55.

opportunities; cooperation towards achievement; involvement in consultation and local democracy; affirmation and questioning of identity; strengthening commitment to place; intercultural links, positive risk-taking – these ... are crucial means of fighting social exclusion. Participation in the arts does this partly by building individual and community competence, but more importantly by building belief in the possibility of positive social change.[27]

Here the magical powers assigned to participation in arts appear as a celebration of culture. But the advocacy of art on the basis of arguments that have nothing to do with it makes art into an instrument of therapeutic propaganda. The very use of the term 'participation' indicates that what is at stake is merely the act of taking part; and since taking part is an end in itself, it matters little what people participate in. It certainly has little to do with art or education. Art can be created by artists, and studied, appreciated or cultivated by others. Education is a process that involves learning, reflection, imagining and engagement with ideas. Neither art nor education are experiences like celebrations, spectacles or elections, in which one participates.

The term participation evokes the spirit of the democratic ideal. But it is a term that needs to be handled with caution. It was noted in Chapter 3 that the meaning of participation is sometimes subverted in the cause of forging an element of interaction with the electorate. E-voting is a striking example of how maintaining the illusion of participation has become the overriding motif. Popular participation is the precondition for ensuring that people have an opportunity to make choices about matters that affect their lives, and it is right that people ought to have a chance to participate in forums that decide how public money is spent on the arts and education. However, exporting

---

[27] F. Matarosso, 'Use or Ornament? The Social Impact of Participation in the Arts', *Comedia*, 1997.

this idea into decision-making about how the arts are run turns the meaning of participation into an empty ritual. 'Cultural inclusion implies allowing people to comment on, even rewrite the stories which museums or others tell us about ourselves' argue advocates of this approach.[28] People are, of course, entitled to rewrite whatever they want, and to transmit their opinions to the cultural elite. The public has an important contribution to make to the world of culture. But whatever contribution it is making, it is not participating in the arts. The public is an audience, at best a critical and educated one. All talk about the 'partnership' between the audience and a cultural institution simply obscures the reality that art is created and produced by artists. Participatory art is nothing more than a public ritual, designed to bind people together through an activity sanctioned by the cultural mandarins. Such activities elevate the taking part and the being there to create the illusion of participation in an activity that actually is beyond the capacity of most of us.

Perpetuating the illusion of participation in art trivializes the artistic experience, and restrains the cultivation of taste and judgement. But its negative consequences pale into insignificance compared to the damage that the promotion of participation in education inflicts on intellectual life. In universities, this process has weakened the line that divides teacher and student. Through the institutionalization of this pseudo-democratic ethos, students are flattered to believe that their view is just as valid as those of their teachers. An environment in which the title 'Teacher' is deprecated and everyone is declared to be a learner, the status of knowledge of a subject is undermined. This caricature of equality between learners undermines the foundation on which the transmission of knowledge can take place. While such an environment may flatter all learners as equal participants in university education, it is at the expense of real learning.

---

[28] Pachter and Landry (2001), p. 97.

The celebration of ordinariness

It can be argued that the project of transforming culture and education into instruments of recognition does no one any harm. In previous times, the ruling powers have used circuses, spectacles, rituals and religions to make people feel good, so what's wrong with turning schools, universities and museums towards that objective? There are two interrelated problems with the institutionalization of recognition through culture and education. It distracts artistic and intellectual life from developing its vision and ideas; and it encourages the conservative impulse of cultural flattery, instead of challenging the public to aspire to a higher level of achievement.

The policy of inclusion through recognition self-consciously attempts to validate people as they are. 'I don't understand how you can speak to people if you don't celebrate their voices', argues the American populist educator Henry Giroux.[29] Unfortunately, the celebration of people's voices is not always consistent with a serious intellectual or aesthetic experience. Education involves challenging people's perception of themselves, calling into question their common sense, and, at its best, demanding that they become something other than what they once were. The institutionalization of recognition makes no demand on people to adopt an active relationship with culture and education, and it discourages them from learning to distinguish between the ordinary and the exceptional.

In practice, the celebration of people's voices turns into the exaltation of the ordinary. The public is conceived of as consisting of ordinary people, whose ordinariness must be cultivated by institutions of culture and education. In Britain, universities are attempting to create an environment that is not alien to the ordinary undergraduate – instead, it should feel like a

[29] Giroux (1992), p. 13.

home away from home. It has been argued that one reason why working-class black youngsters are deterred from applying to Cambridge University is because the city lacks a night life – and so would-be applicants are assured that there is 'plenty of raga, soca and hiphop bands on offer'.[30] In American universities, staff are fully trained in making the ordinary student feel comfortable. Affirmation of the student's voice is a principal theme of the ethos of campus life.

The celebration of ordinariness seeks to endow banality and everyday experience with cultural significance. In a recent exhibition titled 'Telling Lives' at the New York Historical Society, three white-haired ladies sat listening to ordinary people recount their 10-minute stories. After it is finished, a computer prompts the elderly women to tell their stories in front of the camera. According to a review of this exhibition, 'The women are not famous, but they're exactly the reason "Telling Lives" was created.' It appears that recording stories quickly and cheaply provides a large archive of material that can be used in museums and libraries.[31] Talk is not only cheap – it can be readily converted into an object of cultural significance.

Matters are even more complicated when recognition of the ordinary is institutionalized as an automatic right. Recognition as a cultural-political and policy-sanctioned right is consistent with the bureaucratic imperative of treating the individual according to an impersonal general formula. It overlooks individual needs and differences, and fails to distinguish between achievement and failure, wisdom and ignorance. A real recognition of the individual requires that choices are made between knowledge and opinion, and contributions that are worth esteeming and those that are not.

---

[30] Cited in Claire Fox, 'The Massification of Higher Education', in Hayes and Wynyard (2002), p. 138.

[31] Leslie Kandell, 'Stories of the Things That Mattered to You', *New York Times*, 9 November 2003.

Too often the call to celebrate people's voices serves as a euphemism for dishonest flattery. These days the word 'creative' is routinely used to describe any endeavour undertaken by a human being. Educational and cultural projects seek to reassure potential clients that 'we are all creative' and 'we are all special'. It seems that creativity is a characteristic that we are naturally born with. As Peter Jenkinson, director of Creative Partnership, informed the Museum Association conference in October 2003, 'we are all born 100 per cent creative'. No doubt, words of praise and encouragement are useful in motivating people to engage with new experiences. But when praise and encouragement are institutionalized and spoon-fed in a formulaic manner, they serve to demotivate people from putting themselves to the test. There is a fundamental difference between being open to the idea that individual creativity may be achieved by every person and declaring that we are all creative. The promiscuous designation of the label 'creative' overlooks the fact that achievement involves hard work, painful encounters and personal development. Creativity is not a personal characteristic but the outcome of inspired, hard-earned achievement. That is why most of us are not only not special, but too often do not have the opportunity or the inclination to become special. One of the principal casualties of the politics of recognition is commitment to the notion of intellectual and aesthetic development.

Advocates of the institutionalization of recognition regard the demand that people rise to the occasion and prove worthy of the intellectual or artistic experience they encounter as an unreasonable one. From this perspective, the very attempt to maintain academic standards is dismissed as the inflexible attitude of an elite wedded to its narrow privilege. According to this standpoint:

> The fear of diluting academic standards is bound up with the dominant knowledge-centred paradigm. Traditionally, the task is seen as one of inducting students into a certain kind

of elitist academic culture. As a consequence, the institutions of higher education have, on the whole, never felt the need to adapt themselves to students. On the contrary, the assumption has been that students adapted to them on a 'take it or leave it' basis.[32]

The demand that universities adapt to the student inexorably leads to the lowering of expectations. An intellectual challenge by definition confronts all of us with the ultimatum, 'take it or leave it'. The attempt to protect students from tackling this challenge may serve the dogma of inclusion, but only at the expense of weakening cultural support for intellectual development.

The demand that academic standards should adapt to the politics of recognition is paralleled in the arts, where policy makers often stipulate that aesthetic judgements should be subordinated to the agenda of inclusion. The Runnymede Trust argues that the issue of cultural recognition – of whose voice is being heard, and whose representations are being shown – should predominate over artistic judgements. Aesthetics is seen as a mere cover for cultural domination. In its report *The Future of Multi-Ethnic Britain*, the Trust concludes that 'funding and resourcing policies should consciously attend to issues of cultural recognition, identity and belonging, and therefore question many customary criteria of quality and aesthetic value'.[33] The report explicitly acknowledges that what it proposes is 'a major culture change – indeed, a cultural revolution'.[34] This self-conscious marginalization of artistic standards and quality highlights the feeble and philistine foundation on which the policy of recognition is constructed.

The politics of recognition means accepting as valid people's

---

[32] Robin Usher, 'Qualification, Paradigms and Experiential Learning in Higher Education', in Fulton (1989), p. 79.

[33] 'Arts, media and sport', in *The Future of Multi-Ethnic Britain*, 2000, p. 160.

[34] 'Arts, media and sport', in *The Future of Multi-Ethnic Britain*, 2000, p. 166.

accounts of their subjective states. This reluctance to question people's accounts of themselves is reflected by the current climate of cultural relativism. However, the absence of a common moral grammar gives recognition a superficial and provisional character. Recognition without dialogue and critical engagement represents a form of self-validation that tends to promote unstable and defensive identities. Automatic recognition provided by institutions as a matter of routine fails to engage with people's desire to be valued. But by treating recognition as a right formally granted through an institution, it creates a demand for even more guarantees for affirmation.

Recognition accorded through the institutionalization of inclusion represents the cultural flattery of passive subjectivity. Ironically, the institutionalization of the right to recognition necessarily leads to emptying it of any moral content. Recognition that means something to the individual is linked to the sense of achievement. Such a right can never satisfy the craving to be recognized – it merely incites the individual to demand more assurances of respect. But the very act of offering respect to those who crave it may make matters more complicated. As Richard Sennett suggests, the weak may quite rightly experience the extension of such respect as an empty gesture or, worse still, as a ritual confirming their position of inferiority.[35] The celebration of the ordinary rarely succeeds in enthusing its audience. But the problem with the culture of flattery is not simply that it doesn't work. It continually transmits powerful signals that undermine the foundation on which cultural and intellectual life can thrive. Instead of promoting public engagement with the sphere of ideas, it reinforces people's estrangement from this realm.

[35] Sennett (2003).

6   Treating People as Children

Projects collecting oral histories, individual stories, university seminars devoted to undergraduates talking about what's relevant to them, and community exhibitions of people's favourite things are the kind of experiences celebrated by the cult of the ordinary. This celebration of the ordinary is often presented as a democratic, anti-elitist affirmation of the people. This chapter suggests that it is none of that. What it reveals is the patronizing assumptions of the elites that manage institutions of culture and education. Such sentiments are particularly conspicuous in the media, where programmers genuinely believe that ordinary folk have an attention span of three seconds. On both sides of the Atlantic, news organizations searching for the elusive youth market are transforming current events programmes into racy spectacles fit for six-year-olds. Some television broadcasters have expressed alarm at the diminishing quality of their product. Just before his death in the summer of 2003, the veteran newscaster David Brinkley said of the medium that was his life: 'television news has become so trivial and devoid of content as to be little different from entertainment programming'.

Criticism of the direction adopted by the media is invariably dismissed as the knee-jerk reaction of elitist and anti-democratic old fogies who are addicted to the high-brow. But it is not the true spirit of democracy that encourages spoon-feeding culture. The policies of inclusion and affirmation rarely translate into an authentic respect for the wisdom possessed by the intelligent public. It is precisely because the cultural elite has no real respect for people's capacity to improve themselves and to rise to the challenge of the opportunities provided by education and culture that it tends to treat them as potential patients rather than as an audience for ideas. Immunizing school children, university students or museum-goers from feeling intimidated and demoralized might seem an enlightened policy of support. However, by treating people as weak and vulnerable individuals who are likely to stumble when confronted by an intellectual challenge, such cultural attitudes serve to create a climate of low expectations.

Low expectations reveal contempt for those ordinary people who are the target of cultural and educational institutions. As the poet Nicholas Murray asks: 'Does respect for an audience involve appealing to the lowest common denominator, the least demanding performance, the most untaxing pleasure, or does it mean crediting the common reader, the concert goer, the civilised citizen, with some intelligence and appetite for invigorating artistic experience?'[1] A similar question can be posed in relation to the attitude that educational institutions have adopted towards students. Even elite institutions like Harvard University are busy creating an environment where students are treated as fragile children that need to be protected from the risks posed by intellectual disputes and conflict. According to Dorothy Rabinowitz, 'first-year law students can hardly fail to notice the pall of official disapproval now settled over everything smacking of conflict and argument'.[2] A new programme designed for first-year students, 'Managing Difficult Conversations', instructs students on the need to acknowledge emotions in their verbal communication. A publication written by this programme's authors explains in capitals that 'A Difficult Conversation is Anything You Find It Hard to Talk About'. The programme not

---

[1]   Nicholas Murray, 'Culture and Accessibility', in Wallinger and Warnock (2000), pp. 58–9.

[2]   See Dorothy Rabinowitz, 'Difficult Conversations', *The Wall Street Journal*, 19 November 2002.

only infantilizes university students, but also minimizes the role of reason and logic in intellectual debate. It appears that in a 'difficult conversation', which is anything that a person finds hard to talk about, 'logic/reason' has to be combined with 'emotions and personal experience'. If even an elite university like Harvard adopts the mission of instructing young people how to talk about their feelings and experiences, it is not surprising that the more ordinary ones routinely treat their students as confused children.

Infantilized culture

No one actually explicitly supports the process of dumbing down. When institutions adopt a cavalier attitude towards standards they do not do so on the grounds that they want to provide the public with an inferior education or undemanding cultural experience. They do so because they believe that people will feel alienated unless they engage with experiences that are deemed to be directly relevant to their lives and linked to their personal experiences. But inevitably, this emphasis on relevance exists in a state of permanent tension with the acquisition of objective knowledge and an artistic sensibility. Powerful ideas often have an abstract character and are developed through the assimilation of a range of conflicting experiences. That is why they often appear so much at odds with everyday common sense and with the insights gained through personal experience. Acquiring objective knowledge cannot be confined to the process of reflecting on an individual's life story. It also requires a form of education that distances the student from the immediate and everyday, so as to stimulate the mind to imagine other possibilities. There is no direct route from personal emotions to objective knowledge, and students need to be confronted with worlds that are 'irrelevant' to their lives. Sometimes they even have to understand that the knowledge they gained through life is quite irrelevant to their ability to grasp a particular subject.

At some point law students at Harvard will find that acknowledging their emotional and personal experience is not what legal training is about. Studying law requires an understanding of objective facts and their interpretation through forms of reasoning that have little to do with personal experience. It could be argued that the therapeutic encouragement that Harvard students receive need not prevent them from becoming brilliant legal scholars. However, its privileging of the status of personal experience compromises the intellectual horizons of its students. This process can be seen even more clearly in relation to children's education. A recent study of US publishers' guidelines to authors of schoolbook texts makes frightening reading. Guided by the imperative of relevance, these instructions seek to protect children from any references that are remotely distant from their experience. For example, the guidelines advise that a story set in the mountains discriminates against students from flatlands; and one story of a blind mountaineer who climbed to the top of Mount McKinley, the highest peak in North America, was rejected 12-11 by the panel vetting it because of 'regional bias'. It is felt that children should not be expected to read or comprehend stories set in an unfamiliar terrain. Diane Ravitch, the author of this study, notes:

> Consider the impoverishment of imagination that flows from such assumptions: *No reading passage on a test may have a specific geographical setting*: every event should occur in a generic locale. Under these assumptions, no child should be expected to understand a story set in a locale other than the one that he or she currently lives in or a locale that *has no distinguishing characteristics*.[3]

---

[3]   Ravitch (2003), p. 10.

The key point that comes across from Ravitch's text is that the more that school texts have to meet the criterion of relevance, the greater their cultural content is diminished.

The instruction that children living in Switzerland ought not be tested about stories set in a Newfoundland fishing village, or that Asian students should not be examined about stories located in New York, may strike many as a grotesque caricature of an otherwise sound policy of cultural sensitivity. However, most of the more routine policies associated with the ethos of access and relevance are premised upon the same assumptions that have been internalized by the zealous overseers of children's textbooks. From the infant school right through to the university and the museum, the public is continually expected to founder and crumble when entering a cultural terrain that is distant from its own life. Even textbooks targeting university students make an effort to imitate publications aimed at secondary school students: as the content of university courses become more relevant, it has also become less theoretical and less abstract.

The unintended consequence of Harvard University's course on Managing Difficult Conversations, or the publishers' guidelines on school texts, is to infantilize cultural and intellectual life. The significance such initiatives attach to the appearance of relevance and to direct personal experience tends to diminish their intellectual content. At their worst, institutions peddling relevance turn public education and arts into a form of individual therapy that simply affirms rather than teaches or stimulates. Such initiatives are often presented as reflecting a shift towards a more democratic attitude towards culture. They are meant to increase 'participation', 'widen access', 'empower communities', 'break down barriers' and give people an opportunity to express their 'voice'. However these initiatives have little to do with the democratization process. Projects devoted to a more democratic orientation would seek to educate the public to develop its understanding of new and challenging encounters. Instead, these initiatives hope to expand participation by eliminating such challenging encounters, in an attempt to prevent people from being put off by them. As Josie Appleton argues, 'when the new cultural elite talks about breaking down the barriers of culture, in practice this means the reduction of cultural experience to an instant, emotional connection'.[4] She adds that 'reflection and judgment are seen as exclusive, as blocking the connection and shutting people out'.

The infantilization of culture assumes its most distinct character in its elevation of personal experience. When education and culture is treated as the projection of personal sentiment, ideas and objects of art become valued because of their meaning to the individual rather than because of the achievement and importance they represent to the public. A culture that exists in order to help people find themselves fosters a mood of self-obsession and inward orientation. 'This represents a regression to a childlike state, where there is no distinction made between what is of value to me and what is of general value,' notes Appleton.[5] Children tend to value what directly gives them pleasure and affirmation. Cultivating such attitudes amongst the public represents its infantilization. The celebration of the ordinary voice, through the idea that 'this is my story', is not a million miles away from the emotional sentiment that cries out 'this is my toy'.

Infantilizing people

The policies associated with social inclusion and access are based upon a uniquely feeble version of the human subject. In the imagination of the cultural and educational mandarin, the public

---

[4]   Josie Appleton, 'Infantilising Art', forthcoming.
[5]   Josie Appleton, 'Infantilising Art', forthcoming.

lacks the resources to engage with difficult intellectual or artistic encounters, and people are assumed to be incapable of rising to the occasion and overcoming the obstacles they meet. This view transmits the perception that people are children who need to have their hands held as they enter a university campus or pass through the door of a museum or a public library. But the systematic transmission of the idea that people cannot possibly cope when confronted with an intellectual or artistic challenge can have a damaging impact on the public imagination. It is not yet the case that people entering the Metropolitan Museum or the V&A are offered counselling to deal with the intimidating surroundings in which exhibitions are held – however, a young adult becoming a university undergraduate or postgraduate can now access a variety of therapeutic services to help him or her come to terms with the trauma of campus life.

Students confronted with the ordinary troubles of life are routinely advised to seek professional advice and counselling. A change in individual circumstance is often elevated into a problem that requires professional support. Transition counsellors specialize in offering support to individuals embarking on a new phase in their lives. 'The counselling team are fully aware of the importance of managing transition and are here to help you find the way ahead', acclaims the University of Bath Counselling Service on its website. As illustrations of the kind of the transitions that might require professional support, the service mentions entering university as a first-year undergraduate, the move of second-year students from campus-based residence to living in town, final-year students returning after being away on placement, and newly arrived postgraduate students. 'It could be that feelings of self-confidence are quite threatened by the unfamiliarity of new surroundings and new people', warns the service.

Academics too are expected to treat undergraduates as children rather than young men and women. They face continuous pressure to minimize the demands they place on students. In Britain and in the US, university students are often not expected to be able to possess an understanding of grammatical rules or the ability to write an essay. The American Conference for College Composition and Communication, the body that represents professional teachers of this subject, believes that 'if we can convince our students that spelling, punctuation, and usage are less important than content, we [will] have removed a major obstacle in their developing their ability to write'.[6] The exhortation to remove the barriers posed by spelling, punctuation and usage illustrates the kind of education that the access agenda offers to the ordinary student. It is a form of education that is more interested in giving students a sense of achievement than in educating them.

The art of patronizing students is often defined as 'best practice' in universities. Lecturers are required to provide undergraduates with course material that leaves little to chance. The relatively informal student–teacher relationship has been turned into a contractual one. A course outline and reading list is increasingly regarded as a contract that obliges the academic to deliver clearly outlined learning objectives. Students are given handouts to explain what the lecturer is doing. They are frequently provided with lecture notes and with model exam papers that explain how students should answer questions. Lecturers are trained to avoid forms of behaviour that might hurt a student's feelings. Feedback must always be supportive, students should never be told that they are wrong, and examiners must always attempt to find and say something positive about an essay. The style of affirmation favoured by parenting experts for infants has been adopted by the university. Inevitably, the more energy that academics devote to attend to the emotional needs of

---

[6]   Cited in Thomas F. Bertonneau (1996), *Declining Standards at Michigan Public Universities*. Midland, MI: Mackinac Center for Public Policy.

their undergraduates, the less seriously they take them as potential intellectuals.

This process of infantilization expresses a pessimistic and anti-democratic account of people. The target audience of policies of inclusion consists of individuals who bear no resemblance to the ideal of the democratic subject. Ideals of democratic participation presuppose citizens who possess the intelligence and responsibility to act autonomously and exercise their rights. They are able to criticize and take criticism. They possess maturity, a sense of responsibility and are prepared to take an interest in matters that affect not only them but also other sections of their community. Contemporary cultural and educational institutions transmit signals that indicate that people are not expected to behave in accordance with democratic ideals. Instead, they expect their audience to be emotional, only interested in themselves, lacking in curiosity and immature.

Inverted snobbery

From the perspective of our cultural mandarins, anxiety about the intellectual crisis facing the university, the process of dumbing down or the infantilization of the public are entirely misplaced. They believe that all that has happened is that education and culture have become more inclusive, and they interpret the developments criticized in this book as the positive outcome of policies promoting the democratization of culture. As a concept, inclusiveness is presented as an expression of impulses that are anti-elitist and participatory. Hostility to *elitism* is now mandatory for any individual who hopes to join the cultural elite. And the meaning of the term elitist has been expanded to describe language usage, education and cultural experience that is not deemed to be directly relevant or accessible to ordinary people. The language of populism that informs cultural life is informed by a sensibility that regards claims to artistic and intellectual superiority with cynicism. The description of an institution as an elitist one usually contains the sense of disapproval and condemnation. When Oxford or Cambridge are described in such terms, no one is left in any doubt that these are institutions of privilege, dominated by an old-boy network who are out of touch with the aspirations of ordinary folk. The Opera House in Covent Garden symbolizes everything that is said to be wrong with elitist institutions. It is stuffy, expensive, irrelevant and exclusive, and its productions do little to affirm the lives of people living in inner-city London. Worse still, it demands that the audience listens and concentrates for long periods of time to music and songs that are not part of their daily life.

There is of course a sound argument to be made about ensuring that people can afford the price of a ticket to the opera. But criticisms of the opera are not confined to its pricing policy. They express hostility toward the opera as an art form on the grounds that it only engages with the taste of a small elite of privileged men and women. Calls to redirect expenditure on opera to regional theatres or community art centres are often linked to expressions of cultural preference. The supposedly bold and innovative productions of a community interactive theatre are favourably contrasted to the allegedly lifeless and irrelevant opera patronized by the privileged elite. The language of philistinism employed in such debates has led one commentator to write about today's 'elite of anti-elitists'.[7]

It is important to realize that the institutionalization of anti-elitist sentiment is not a response to the assertion of popular culture from below. It is not ordinary folk who are in the vanguard of the campaign to transform education and culture to one that is deemed accessible and relevant. Anti-elitism is a cause that has emerged from within the elite itself. It can be most

[7]   Walden (2001), p. 43.

usefully seen as a form of snobbishness – or, more precisely, as inverted snobbery.

A snob is traditionally defined as one whose ideas and conduct are prompted by vulgar admiration for wealth and social position. Inverted snobbery is motivated by an uncritical embrace of the ordinary and the popular. Inverted snobs are uncritically critical of forms of culture that were valued and cultivated in the past. What they object to is not the aesthetic content of a particular art form, but the fact that it is old and was produced or appreciated by the wrong type of people. The main targets of inverted snobs are the elites who are still self-consciously elitist, and their elitism is regarded as a sin with unpardonable consequences. This is a very different critique of elitism than that which was mounted by progressive movements in the past. The target of nineteenth- and twentieth-century progressive movements was elite privilege and the determination of the oligarchy to control and monopolize society's resources at the expense of the quality of life of the majority. Anti-elitism today is rarely focused on economic power. Rather, its fire is directed against forms of behaviour, culture and education that are often wrongly associated with the elite. Sophisticated language, complex ideas, challenging education, and demanding art forms are today stigmatized as elitist and therefore deemed to be a bad thing. The very claim to standards of excellence can be represented as elitist since, by implication, it disrespects those whose achievements fail to match it. Protecting people from elitist culture is seen as mandatory, since such culture is seen as a threat to the self-esteem of ordinary people.

The anti-elitist stance of the elites has had a profound impact on intellectual life. These attitudes have distracted intellectuals and cultural producers from developing their work in directions that are not directly relevant to the demands of everyday routine. Although intellectuals and artists do their best to develop their work, they continually face institutional pressure to fall in line with current policies. Political compulsion and calculations have always represented a challenge for genuine intellectual work or artistic endeavour. The current era is no exception to this trend. Today there is great pressure upon academics, educators and cultural producers to buy into the populist dogma that has been constructed by anti-elitist elites. As one proponent of the populist turn argues, 'today, a code of intellectual activism which is not grounded in the vernacular of information technology and the discourses and images of popular commercial culture is likely to be ineffective'.[8]

The different manifestations of inverted snobbery often appear as an affectation adopted by a manipulative elite. It is certainly difficult to take powerful and wealthy cultural mandarins seriously when they argue the case for eliminating elitist privilege and extending the agenda of inclusion. Some commentators take the view that the elites do not really mean what they say in relation to culture and education. This standpoint is forcibly argued by the transatlantic critic Christopher Hitchens, who believes that 'populism' has become 'the main tactical weapon, the main vernacular of elitism'. He adds that 'certainly the most successful elitist in American culture now, American politics, is the most successful inventor or manipulator, or leader of populism'.[9]

Hitchens is right to alert us to the top-down character of populist trends in contemporary culture. But the anti-elitism of the cultural elite is not simply an affectation adopted for the purposes of public consumption. It reflects genuine sentiments of an elite that lacks conviction about its own status and authority. When privileged white men who run American universities, or British mandarins who manage the BBC, disparage dead white

---

[8]   Ross (1989), p. 212
[9]   See Christopher Hitchens, 'The Future of the Public Intellectual', *The Nation*, 12 February 2001.

men they are semi-consciously expressing their own contempt for their own personal positions. When graduates of Harvard and Oxford denounce elitist educational institutions they reveal a profound sense of unease about transmitting to society the values that they had internalized in their youth. Unable to rest their authority on the institutions and conventions that have secured their position, they are in the business of searching for an alternative source of legitimacy. In a sense, they have become estranged from the institutions and values that provided the platform on which they built their careers.

The lack of affirmation for the elite's authority has led to a situation where the elite finds it difficult to summon up conviction in its own mission. It does not possess any strong beliefs, and therefore is open to negotiation about what should be valued and ought to be rejected. It has sought to overcome the dilemma posed by its own crisis of belief by declaring that no beliefs can claim to possess a monopoly on truth. That is why the cultural elite is so susceptible to the influence of cultural relativism. Its estrangement from a sense of mission and lack of clarity about truth with a capital T has encouraged a flexible attitude toward values and truth. By putting a question mark against all previously held values and institutions, the elite avoids the necessity of coming up with the answers about what beliefs and practices society ought to value and uphold. Instead of giving answers, it provides recognition and affirmation. The populist policies of inclusion and affirmation help the elite to evade replying to questions for which it has no unambiguous answers.

The elite's loss of conviction in its own authority is most strikingly reflected in the sphere of politics. But it has also had a formidable impact on culture and education. It has helped fuel a process of disorientation, which has undermined the elite's capacity to transmit a clear vision of its objectives. Policy makers, museum directors and university administrators are genuinely uncertain about standards and dubious about the value of maintaining them. Not only are they unwilling to affirm their cultural legacy – they also find it difficult to discriminate between the quality and value of popular entertainment and ideas and works that are the products of genuine intellectual innovation and artistic creativity.

What we have is a disoriented cultural elite that lacks firm convictions and feels unable to project a coherent picture of the world to the rest of society. It is an elite that feels uncomfortable with the idea of self-consciously acting as an elite. Aware of its own incoherence as a group, it does not dare claim to possess attributes of distinctiveness and superiority. Unable to assert itself as a cultural elite, it declares that, in any case, it is wrong to try to improve and educate people; and that not only does it have nothing to teach but it also has a lot to learn from ordinary folk. This apparent reversal of the relationship between elite and people is clearly expressed through the process of inverted snobbery. It is important to underline the word 'apparent' because its current embrace of the people coincides with belief that the public is incapable of engaging with demanding intellectual and cultural encounters. Hence the paradoxical situation in which the celebration of the ordinary coexists with a lack of belief in the capacity of the public to handle sophisticated and complex ideas.

The low expectations that society's institutions have adopted towards the public is a unique feature of our times. Historically, the attitude of the elites towards the public has undergone a number of significant changes.

In pre-modern times, the elites took the view that the public was not capable of understanding Truth and lacked the capacity to grasp profound insights. The opinion of Plato's Socrates that 'it is impossible that a multitude be philosophic' was rarely challenged by the intellectuals of antiquity and pre-modern times. One of the important legacies of the Enlightenment was to challenge this representation of the public. The majority of Enlightenment thinkers continued to have a low opinion of the intellectual capacity of the public to reason, and believed that the ability to think scientifically was confined to members of the elite. However, these thinkers also took the view that it was possible to educate and gradually enlighten the multitudes. From the middle of the nineteenth century, the belief that the elite had a duty to enlighten the people gained strength. This was a project readily embraced by the modern intellectual, and continued to motivate the cultural elites until the 1970s.

One of the distinctive features of the contemporary so-called postmodern era is the loss of conviction in the idea that the public is capable of being enlightened. But scepticism about the project of public enlightenment is rarely expressed in a coherent and explicit form. In an era of inclusion and participation, doubts about the capacity of people cannot be raised in a clear and open manner. We live in an era where clear statements about people's ability are obfuscated by a vocabulary that relies on terms like 'special needs students', 'differently abled people', 'non-traditional students', and 'the intellectually challenged'. This confusing language coexists with the rhetoric of flattery that declares that everyone is special and creative. But at a time when normal university students are routinely described as vulnerable, it is evident that the mental capacity of the public is not held in high esteem.

The flattery of people allows the cultural elite to avoid assuming its traditional role toward the public. Since people are apparently so creative and their ordinary lives provide so many important insights, it would be pointless and arrogant for an elite to assume the burden of enlightening the public. Instead of cultivating the public imagination, the role of the cultural elite becomes to validate and celebrate it. The policy of recognition allows the Establishment to forge a point of contact with people, and also to avoid confronting the crisis of its legitimacy.

The contradictory relationship of today's cultural elite to the public is resolved through the argument that there is something inherently wrong in teaching, instructing or cultivating the taste of the public. This sentiment has acquired the status of an incontrovertible truth among opinion-makers. A report written for the British Arts Council expressed the argument in the following terms:

> Too often in the past, the arts have taken a patronizing attitude to audiences. Too often artists and performers have continued to ply their trade to the same white, middle-class audience. In the back of their minds lurks the vague hope that one day enlightenment might descend semi-miraculously upon the rest, that the masses might get wise to their brilliance.[10]

Under the guise of condemning elitism, the report questions the very idea that artists or intellectuals can have a role in enlightening people. According to this cynical view, the public has little to learn and institutions of culture should get into the business of recognizing this fact.

The construction of a docile public

The cumulative impact of the politics of recognition is the construction of a docile and conformist public. Institutions of culture and education treat the people as consumers who have culture and education spoon-fed to them. The cultural regime of low expectations does little to stimulate public discussion and debate. And in any case, the diminished importance attached to ideas and scepticism towards the status of knowledge means that there is little point in taking such debates too seriously. The absence of culturally affirmed standards deprives people of a common language through which they can make judgements of value and gain coherence as a public. Debate and rational

[10] Cited in Walden (2001), p. 108.

argument over the vital issues of the day is difficult in a society that is devoted to the celebration of individual voices.

An intelligent public is the product of intellectual and cultural ferment and intense debate. As the American sociologist C. Wright Mills has argued, the public is distinguished by its ability to develop its arguments and to express them in society. 'In a *public* as I understand the term, virtually as many people express opinions as receive them; public communications are so organised that there is a chance immediately and effectively to answer back to any opinion expressed in public,' observes Wright Mills.[11] Wright Mills places particular emphasis on autonomy and independence from official institutions as one of the preconditions for the functioning of a flourishing public, and has clearly counterposed a public which is 'more or less autonomous in its operation' to what he called *the mass*. In a mass, far fewer people express theirs opinion than receive them. Communications are organized in such a manner that it is difficult for people to 'answer back or with effect'. Most important of all, 'the mass has no autonomy from institutions; on the contrary, agents of authorized institutions interpenetrate this mass, reducing any autonomy it may have in the formation of opinion by discussion'.[12]

Today's cultural climate is more hospitable to the development of a mass than to a public. Argument and debate are often represented as adversarial and damaging. The growth of scepticism and of cultural relativism calls into question the value of battling over ideas. When there is little at stake, debate may seem pointless. But probably the most significant development that serves to undermine the workings of the public is the expansion of official and semi-official institutions into cultural

[11]   C. Wright Mills, 'Mass Society and Liberal Education', in Horowitz (1963), p. 355.

[12]   C. Wright Mills, 'Mass Society and Liberal Education', in Horowitz (1963), p. 355.

and intellectual life. The massive expansion of the university, the rise of credentialism and the growing intervention of the state in cultural life have reduced the terrain on which the public can exercise its autonomy. Policies which fly the flags of inclusion, access and participation often lead to the penetration of official institutions into people's lives. The auditing of cultural institutions and of the relationship between students and academics tends to compromise informal and spontaneous interaction. Through a variety of devices – lifelong learning, certificates of competence, training and development – people's intellectual and cultural life becomes subject to institutional expectations. These trends stimulate a mood of conformism and passivity.

The imperative of social engineering leads to the colonization of people's informal lives. The accreditation of prior learning is presented as an acknowledgement of the important learning experiences that people have acquired through their encounters in their communities and at work. And many people are delighted that their lives are taken seriously by educators. At a recent academic conference, one woman reported just how pleased she was that her previous life as a housewife was accredited and deemed as relevant to her course. But do we really want our lives to be accredited and certificated by an institution? The formalization of personal experience through institutional recognition has a corrosive impact on the public, and inevitably weakens its autonomy. Accreditation leads to the auditing of personal experience according to criteria established by an external institution. It always contains the potential for forcing the public into a relationship of subservience to the auditors.

The social engineering agenda self-consciously seeks to colonize the life-world of the public. For example, a report written to justify the merits of small museums claims that the strength of small museums lies in 'terms of the impact they can have on individuals and to a lesser extent, whole communities (e.g. enhancing self-esteem, skills development, recuperative

benefits)'. Why? Because they can forge more 'intimate relationships with individual community members' and assist 'the
creation of networks of friends and other social contacts for
elderly people'.[13] Invading the sphere of informal relations is one
of the desired outcomes of this project.

Final thoughts

The trivialization of the public's cultural potential has important
implications for the future of intellectual thought. Intellectuals
need an intelligent public and artists need an engaged critical
audience. Unfortunately, the politics of cultural flattery create
little incentive for people to rise to the occasion. As a result, the
pool of society's creative energy is wasted on creating and
responding to the demand for recognition. Those who insist on
undertaking a genuine journey of intellectual discovery risk being
labelled as elitist and irrelevant. 'I've increasingly become
convinced that in order to be any kind of a public intellectual
commentator or combatant, one has to be unafraid of the charges
of elitism,' writes Christopher Hitchens.[14] Anyone who is
genuinely concerned with the disturbing influences that dominate
our cultural life would find it difficult to disagree with Hitchens's
sentiment.

Intellectuals inside and outside the university, and their
colleagues in the world of culture and the arts, must face up to
the uncomfortable truth that they risk making themselves
irrelevant if they allow current institutional pressures to dominate
their work. Some of us have actively internalized the politics of
cultural flattery while others have sought an easy life by

---

[13] See *www.resource.gov.uk/documents/lat325* v2.pdf.
[14] See Christopher Hitchens, 'The Future of the Public Intellectual', *The
Nation*, 12 February 2001.

acquiescing in institutional demands. Intellectuals need to reconstitute themselves through reclaiming the autonomy for which their predecessors fought in previous times. Such autonomy can best be constructed by engaging with the public's own aspiration to be taken seriously, and helping to cultivate that aspiration. In an era of the infantilization of culture, treating people as grown-ups has become one of the principal duties of the humanist intellectual.

A lot has been said about the corrosive impact of cultural policies, particularly those of social inclusion, on the quality of contemporary intellectual life. But it would be wrong to put the blame entirely upon governments and cultural institutions. Politicians and public institutions have always attempted to impose their agenda on culture and education, and elected representatives have every right to be interested in the workings of publicly funded institutions. What is worrying is not the role of the political class so much as the compliance of the world of art and education with a philistine social engineering agenda. Nor has all the pressure towards dumbing down come from outside the academy or the arts. The culture of flattery has for long been internalized by educators and cultural producers. Relativist epistemologies and contempt for standards have been endowed with intellectual credibility by academic practitioners. So there do not appear to be many obvious candidates who come out well from this story.

In as much as it means anything, dumbing down does not refer to the intelligence of people. Rather it is a statement about culture – more specifically, about the elites who influence and regulate the flow of cultural ideas. There is very little that we can do to force the elites to give up their instrumentalist and philistine world view. But we can wage a battle of ideas for the hearts and minds of the public. How we do it is one of the key questions of our time.

Bibliography

Alexander, J. C. and Sztompka, P. (eds) (1990) *Rethinking Progress*. Boston, MA: Unwin Hyman.

Appleton, J. (2001) *Museums for 'The People'?* London: Academy of Ideas.

Arendt, H. (1993) *Between Past and Future*. New York: Penguin.

Barnett, R. (1990) *The Idea of Higher Education*. Buckingham: Open University Press.

Bauman, Z. (1987) *Legislators and Interpreters: On Modernity, Postmodernity and Intellectuals*. Cambridge: Polity Press.

Bauman, Z. (1991) *Modernity and the Holocaust*. Cambridge: Polity Press.

Beck, U. (1992) *Risk Society: Towards a New Modernity*. London: Sage.

Beck, U., Giddens, A. and Lash, S. (eds) (1994) *Reflexive Modernisation: Politics, Tradition and Aesthetics in the Modern Social Order*. Cambridge: Polity Press.

Benda, J. (1959) *The Betrayal of the Intellectuals*. Boston, MA: The Beacon Press.

Berman, M. (2001) *The Twilight of American Culture*. New York: Norton.

Berube, M. (1994) *Public Access: Literary Theory and American Cultural Politics*. London: Verso.

Bourdieu, P. (1988) *Homo Academicus*. Cambridge: Polity Press.

Coser, L. A. (1965) *Men of Ideas: A Sociologist's View*. New York: The Free Press.

Cowen, T. (2000) *In Praise of Commercial Culture*. Cambridge, MA: Harvard University Press.

Debray, R. (1981) *Teachers, Writers, Celebrities; The Intellectuals of Modern France*. London: Verso.

Department of Culture, Media and Sport (2000) *Centres For Social Change: Museums, Galleries and Archives for All. Policy guidance on social inclusion for DCMS funded and local authority museums, galleries and archives in England*. London: DCMS.

Eyerman, R. (1994) *Between Culture and Politics; Intellectuals in Modern Society*. Cambridge: Polity Press.

Eyerman, R., Svensson, L. G. and Soderqvist, T. (eds) (1987) *Intellectuals, Universities, and the State in Western Modern Societies*. Berkeley, CA: University of California Press.

Fairclough, N. (2000) *New Labour, New Language?* London: Routledge.

Fink, L., Leonard, S. T. and Reid, D. M. (eds) (1996) *Intellectuals and Public Life; Between Radicalism and Reform*. Ithaca, NY: Cornell University Press.

Fulton, O. (ed.) (1989) *Access and Institutional Change*. Milton Keynes: Open University Press.

Furedi, F. (1992) *Mythical Past, Elusive Future; History and Society in an Anxious Age*. London: Pluto Press.

Furedi, F. (2003) *Therapy Culture: Cultivating Vulnerability in an Anxious Age*. London: Routledge.

Gagnon, A. G. (1987) *Intellectuals in Liberal Democracies; Political Influence and Social Involvement*. New York: Praeger.

Gerth, H. H. and Wright Mills, C. (1958) *From Max Weber: Essays in Sociology*. New York: Oxford University Press.

Giner, S. (1976) *Mass Society*. London: Martin Robertson.

Giroux, H. (1992) *Border Crossings: Cultural Workers and the Politics Of Education*. London: Routledge.

Gouldner, A. W. (1979) *The Future of Intellectuals and the Rise of the New Class*. London: Macmillan Press.

Graham, G. (2002) *Universities: The Recovery of an Idea*. Thorverton: Imprint Academic.

Halsey, A. H. (1992) *Decline of Donnish Dominion: The British Academic Professions in the Twentieth Century*. Oxford: Clarendon Press.

Hayek, F. A. (ed.) (1954) *Capitalism and the Historians*. London: Routledge & Kegan Paul.

Hayek, F. A. (1978) *Three Sources of Human Values*. London: London School of Economics.

Hayes, D. and Wynyard, R. (eds) (2002) *The McDonaldization of Higher Education*. Westport, CT: Bergin & Harvey.

Horowitz, I. L. (ed.) (1963) *Power, Politics and People: The Collected Essays of C. Wright Mills*. London: Oxford University Press.

Huszar, De G. B. (ed.) (1960) *The Intellectuals: A Controversial Portrait*. Glencoe: The Free Press.

Illich, I., Zola, K. I., McKnight, R., Caplan, J. and Shaiken, H. (1977) *Disabling Professions*. New York: Marion Boyars.

Jacoby, R. (1987) *The Last Intellectuals; American Culture in the Age of Academe*. New York: Basic Books.

Jowell, R., Curtice, J., Park, A. *et al.* (eds) (1995) *British Social Attitudes: The 12th Report*. Dartmouth: SCPR.

Koestler, A. (1983) *The Yogi and the Commissar and Other Essays*. London: Hutchinson.

Lasch, C. (1966) *The New Radicalism In America [1889–1963]: The Intellectual as a Social Type*. London: Chatto & Windus.

Leavis, F. R. (1965) *Educations and the University: A Sketch for an English School*. London: Chatto & Windus.

Leavis, Q. D. (1968) *Fiction and the Reading Public*. London: Chatto & Windus.

Lipset, S. M. (1960) *Political Man*. London: Mercury Books.

Luhman, N. (1993) *Risk: A Sociological Theory*. New York: Walter de Gruyter.

Lyotard, J.-F. (1984) *The Postmodern Condition: A report on knowledge*. Minneapolis: University of Minnesota Press.

Mackenzie, G. and Labiner, J. (2002) *Opportunity Lost: The Decline of Trust and Confidence in Government after September 11*. Washington DC: Center for Public Services.

Matarosso, F. (1997) *The Social Impact of Participation in the Arts*. London: Comedia.

Mattick Jr, P. (1986) *Social Knowledge: An Essay on the Nature and Limits of Social Science*. London: Hutchinson.

Melzer, A. M., Weinberger, J. and Zinman, M. R. (2003) *The Public Intellectual: Between Philosophy and Politics*. Lanham, NJ: Rowman & Littlefield.

Michael, J. (2000) *Anxious Intellects: Academic Professionals, Public Intellectuals and Enlightenment Values*. Durham, NC: Duke University Press.

Minihan, J. (2001) *The Nationalisation of Culture*. London: Hamish Hamilton.

Novick, P. (1988) *That Noble Dream: 'The Objectivity Question' and the American Historical Profession*. Cambridge: Cambridge University Press.

Orwell, G. (1941) *The Lion and the Unicorn*. London: Secker & Warburg.

Pachter, M. and Landry, C. (2001) *Culture at the Crossroads; Culture and Cultural Institutions at the beginning of the 21st Century*. London: Comedia.

Parry, M. and Wake, C. (eds) (1990) *Access and Alternative Futures for Higher Education*. London: Hodder & Stoughton.

Parsons, T. (1954) *Essays in Sociological Theory*. New York: The Free Press of Glencoe.

Pells, R. H. (1985) *The Liberal Mind in a Conservative Age: American Intellectuals in the 1940s and 1950s*. New York: Harper & Row.

Phillips, M. (1998) *All Must Have Prizes*. London: Warner Books.

Purdy, J. (1999) *For Common Things: Irony, Trust and Commitment in America Today*. New York: Alfred A. Knopf.

Rahe, P. (2003) 'The Idea of the Public Intellectual in the Age of the Enlightenment', in Melzer, Weinberger and Zinman (2003).

Revitch, D. (2003) *Language Police: How Pressure Groups Restrict What Students Learn*. New York: Alfred A. Knopf.

Robbins, B. (ed.) (1990) *Intellectuals, Aesthetics, Politics, Academics*. Minneapolis: University of Minnesota Press.

Robbins, B. (1993) *Secular Vocations: Intellectuals, Professionalism, Culture*. London: Verso.

Ross, A. (1989) *No Respect; Intellectuals and Popular Culture*. New York: Routledge.

Said, E. (1994) *Representations of the Intellectual*. London: Vintage.

Sennett, R. (2003) *Respect: The Formation of Character in an Age of Inequality*. New York: Norton.

Shils, E. (1972) *The Intellectuals and the Powers and Other Essays*. Chicago: University of Chicago Press.

Shorter Oxford English Dictionary, The (1965). Oxford: Clarendon Press.

Small, H. (ed.) (2002) *The Public Intellectual*. Oxford: Blackwell Publishing.

Spender, D. and Sarah, E. (1992) *Learning to Lose; Sexism and Education.* New York: Women's Press.

Stout, M. (2000) *The Feel-Good Curriculum; The Dumbing-Down of America's Kids in the Name of Self-Esteem.* Boston, MA: Perseus Books.

Strahern, M. (ed.) (2000) *Audit Cultures.* London: Routledge.

Tusa, J. (2003) *On Creativity; Interviews Exploring the Process.* London: Methuen.

Walden, G. (2001) *The New Elites: Making a Career in the Masses.* London: Penguin Books.

Wallinger, M. and Warnock, M. (eds) (2000) *Art for All? Their Policies and Our Culture.* London: Peer.

Young, M. (1961) *The Rise of the Meritocracy, 1870–2033: An Essay on Education and Equality.* Harmondsworth: Penguin Books.

Articles

Aronowitz, S. (2003) 'A Mills Revival?', *Logos* 2(3) (Summer 2003).

Berman, R. A. (1989) 'Perestroika for the University!', *Telos* 81 (Fall).

Bourdieu, P. (1989) 'The Corporatism of the Universal: The Role of Intellectuals in the Modern World', *Telos* 81 (Fall).

Brouwer, D. C. and Squires, C. R. (2003) 'Public Intellectuals, Public Life, And The University', *Argumentation and Advocacy* 39.

Gamson, W. A. (1999) 'Beyond the Science-versus-Advocacy Distinction', *Contemporary Sociology* 28(1).

Heinrich, K. (1989) 'The Spiritual Impoverishment of the German University', *Telos* 81 (Fall).

Karnoouh, C. (1989) 'Notes on the Crisis of the University', *Telos* 81 (Fall).

Luke, T. (1998) 'Miscast canons? The Future of Universities in an Era of Flexible Specialization', *Telos* 111 (Spring).

Pan, D. (1998) 'The Crisis of the Humanities and the End of the University', *Telos* 111 (Spring).

Piccone, P. (1989) 'The Reuniversalization of the University', *Telos* 81 (Fall).

Piccone, P. (1998) 'The End of Public Education?', *Telos* 111 (Spring).

Index

academic freedom   76–7, 102–3
access movement   67, 95–6,
    100–1, 110, 114–17
accreditation of prior learning
    66–8, 154
aesthetics   135
Alexander, Jeffrey   55
American Conference for College
    Composition and
    Communication   144
Amis, Kingsley   99
Anderson, Amanda   75
Appleton, Josie   97, 142
Arendt, Hannah   111–12
Aristotle   4
Arnold, Matthew   3
artistic activity   13–14, 147–8
Arts Council   105, 128, 152
auditing   107–8, 154
autonomy
    institutional   100–2, 106–7,
        110–11
    intellectual   32–3, 43, 49
    of the public from institutions
        153–4

banality in cultural life   8–10, 25,
    133
Bank of England monetary policy
    committee   6–7
Barnett, Ron   5, 68
Bath University Counselling
        Service   143
Bauman, Z.   32, 36, 45
Bazalgette, Peter   89
BBC   16, 81, 148–9
Beck, Ulrich   57–8
Benda, Julien   28
Benjamin, George   6
Berman, Morris   55
Berman, Russell   76, 101
Big Brother   83–4, 88–9
Blackstone, Tessa   15
Blair, Cherie   82
Blair, Tony   74, 89
Bloom, Alan   61
Bloomsbury set   27
books, study of   1–2
Bourdieu, Pierre   32, 34, 102–4,
    107
Bradford Cathedral   119
Brent East by-election (2003)   79
Brinkley, David   137
British Broadcasting
    Corporation   *see* BBC
Brookings Institution   80–1
Brouwer, D.C.   42
Burke, Edmund   27
Bush, George W.   73, 82, 90
business values   108–9

Cambridge University   6–7, 133,
    146
change, attitudes to   54–8

China 59
citizenship education 124
Clarke, Charles 2–4
Classical Theater Lab 94
Cleveland, Ohio 104
Clinton, Bill 73, 82
Coleman, Stephen 88–9
Collini, Stefan 9–10, 118–19
commercial pressures 15, 104, 109, 112–13; *see also* market forces
Commission for Architecture and the Built Environment 96
Committee for the Study of the American Electorate 78
conformity
  intellectual 46–9, 104
  of the public 152, 154
consumerism 110
Coser, Lewis 31, 35
Cotton, John 27
Covent Garden Opera House 146
Cowen, Tyler 111
creativity 33–4, 113, 125, 134
credentialism 43, 154
Cruise O'Brien, Conor 53
cultural values and truths 6
culture
  attitudes to 4
  autonomy of 100
  high and low 5–6, 93
  relevance and accessibility of 93–4, 139–41
  see also popular culture
Culture Wars 15

Davis, Gray 80
Debray, Regis 35
democratization of intellectual

and cultural life 19, 23, 145
Department for Culture, Media and Sport (DCMS) 96, 100, 103, 106, 115, 128
Department for Education 124
detachment, intellectual 34
devolution 79
'difficult conversations' 138–9, 141
Disneyfication 118
Douglas, Stephen 73
dumbing down vii, 10–15, 24, 74, 80, 84, 90, 95, 111, 116, 119, 121, 139, 145, 156
Duncan Smith, Iain 74

Ecclestone, Kathryn 127
Einstein, Albert 4, 32
election turnout 77–9, 84–7
elitism 6, 14, 19–20, 23–4, 67, 89, 91, 96, 99–101, 118–21, 129, 137–8, 150–1, 155–6
  opposition to 145–9, 152
emotional needs 123–4, 144–5
empowerment 126
Enlightenment philosophy 13, 27, 30, 34–5, 43–7, 150–1
  opposition to 52–62, 69
Enron Corporation 82
equality of opportunity 17–18, 99
essay-writing 95
Establishment, the 151
Evans, Mary 7
Evans, Matthew 93
examination system 17
experiential learning 64–8
expertise, academic 41
Eyerman, Ron 31–3, 40–1, 44

failure, sense of   21–2, 123
Fairclough, Norman   126
'feel-good curriculum'   123–4
feminism   62–3
Le Figaro   80
Foucault, Michel   4, 45, 47
freedom of speech   76
French Revolution   54
Fridjonsdottir, Katrin   37, 39, 41

Gallagher, Noel   6
Gallup polls   80–1
Giddens, Anthony   57–8
Gilligan, Carole   63
Giroux, Henry   132
Gladstone, W.E.   118–20
Goethe, J.W. von   3
Gore, Al   73
Gouldner, Alvin   29–32, 38
Grafton, Anthony   11
Graham, Gordon   102–3, 115–16
Gronewalter, Michael   90
Guggenheim Museum,
    Bilbao   12
Gyroscope Inc.   118

Haber, Stephen   76
Hansard Society   88
Harvard University   138–41, 149
Hassner, Pierre   72
higher education, developments
    in   65–8, 97–101, 109–10,
    120
Hitchens, Christopher   148, 155
Hofstadter, Richard   27
Holocaust, the   56–7
humanism   52–3, 156

idealism   32, 42
identity politics   125

inclusion   17, 24, 84–9, 95, 110,
    116–21, 124–8, 131–2, 135–6,
    145, 148
  through affirmation   120–1,
    126–8, 149
  see also social exclusion and
    inclusion
Institute of Ideas   vii
Institute for Learning and Teaching
    in Higher Education   116
institutionalization of intellectual
    activity   40–2, 49
instrumentalism   2–3, 12–14, 20,
    69, 92, 100, 103–4, 110, 112,
    156
intellectuals
  autonomy of   32–3, 43, 49
  concept and definition of
    31–9, 44
  conformity of   46–9
  conservative and *radical*   35, 46
  as *legislators* and as *interpreters*
    45
  specificity of   45
  status and influence of   26–31,
    38, 43–6, 52, 72
  traditional   37–8, 43
Internet resources   52, 87–9
inverted snobbery   146–50
Iraq war (2003)   83

Jacoby, Russell   31
Jenkins, Peter   55
Jenkinson, Peter   134
Jouvenel, Bertrand de   29, 108

Kakutani, Michiko   74
Kennedy, John F.   73
knowledge
  authority of   65–9, 72, 75

knowledge, *continued*
 fear of 56
 for its own end 69
 personal 65-6
 societal attitudes to 50-9, 64
'knowledge society' and
 'knowledge economy' 6-7,
 11
Koestler, Arthur 28

Lasch, Christopher 21-2
law, study of 140
'learning outcomes' 76-7
Leavis, F.R. 15
Lewisham Council 85
libraries 96-7
Library and Information
 Commission 127-8
lifelong learning 127
Lincoln, Abraham 73
Lipset, Seymour 36
Luhmann, Nikolas 58
Luxemburg, Rosa 4
Lyotard, Jean-François 7

McDonaldization 115-16
Machlup, Fritz 63-4
Maistre, Joseph de 54
managerialism 2, 73, 83
market forces 41, 43, 108-12,
 116; *see also* commercial
 pressures
Marx, Karl 3
mass entertainment 111-12
Mattick, P. Jr 63
Medrano, Maery ta 118
Mental Health Foundation 124
meritocratic ideal 18-22
Metropolitan Museum, New York
 105, 143

Millennium Dome 12, 119
Montebello, Philippe de 105
Murray, Nicholas 138
museums 93, 97, 114-15,
 118-19, 121, 128-9, 154-5

Nabar, Vrinda 3
National Health Service 98-9
National Museums of Scotland
 121
New Labour 73, 79, 82, 126
New Left thinking 61
New York Historical Society 133
Newman, John Henry 69
news on television 137
Nietzsche, Friedrich 3, 56, 61
Nixon, Richard 73
Northern Ireland Executive 129
Novick, P. 63
Nunokawa, Jeff 75

objective knowledge 5-8, 60-2,
 68-70, 139
opera 146
ordinariness, celebration of
 132-7, 150
Orwell, George 8, 34
Oxford University 6-7, 146, 149

Parsons, Talcott 12
participation, nature of 87-9,
 92, 97-9, 120, 130-1, 141-2,
 145
paternalism 23-4, 118
Paulin, Tom 76
Pells, R.H. 25
Perot, Ross 73
philistinism 2-3, 10, 20, 24, 64,
 70-2, 93, 103, 111, 135, 146,
 156

Phillips, Melanie   123
Plato   150
policy action teams (PATs)   106
politics
   disengagement from   77–88
   standards of debate   72–4
politicians, trust in   80–1
popular culture   99
populism   88–9, 92–4, 110, 119,
      145–9
postmodernism   43–6, 62, 64,
      151
pragmatism in pursuit and use of
      knowledge   69–71
professionalism and
      professionalization   38–43,
      48–9
Proust, Marcel   27
Purdy, Jedediah   125

qualifications   17
Quirk, Barry   85

Rabinowitz, Dorothy   138
Rahe, Paul A.   30
rationalism   53–7
Ravitch, Diane   140–1
Raynsford, Nick   86–7
reality television   83–4, 88
relativism   4–5, 16–17, 60–4,
      68–9, 75–6, 136, 149, 153,
      156
Rintoul, Gordon   121
risk   57–60
Ritzer, George   115
Robbins, Bruce   48–9
Romero, A.   16
Ross, Andrew   47–8
Runnymede Trust   135
Ruskin, John   117

Saatchi and Saatchi   115
Said, Edward   34, 36, 39
Sarah, Elizabeth   65
scholarship   2–4
Schopenhauer, Arthur   56
Schumpeter, Joseph   28–9
Schwarzenegger, Arnold   80
Scott, Peter   109–10
self-esteem   123–4, 147
Selwood, Sara   106
Sennett, Richard   136
September 11th 2001, aftermath
      of   81, 105
Shakespeare, William   94
sleaze   81–2
Small, H.   48
Smith, Chris   5–6
Smout, Christopher   121
Social Darwinism   61
social engineering   93–4, 98–100,
      103, 119, 129, 154, 156
   and the market   108–13
social exclusion and inclusion
      97–100, 105–6, 109, 112–14,
      119–29, 142, 156
Socrates   150
soundbites   72, 74
Soviet Union   59
specialization, intellectual   70–1
Spender, Dale   65
Squires, C.R.   42
standards of excellence   14–20,
      23–4, 99, 113, 134–5, 147, 156
   hostility towards   16–17
   negotiation of   15–18
stock exchanges   63–4
Stout, Maureen   123–4
student-centred education   68,
      116–17
subjective experience   65

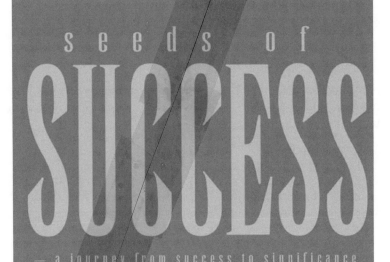

seeds of

SUCCESS

— a journey from success to significance

Bill & Billy Moyer

foreword by: Paul J. Meyer
New York Times Best-Selling Author

The
**LEADING
EDGE**
**Publishing
Company**

Seeds of Success

A Journey from Success to Significance

Published by The Leading Edge Publishing Company
PO Box 7411
Waco, TX 76714
www.theleadingedgepublishing.com

Cover design: Damien Mayfield
Interior design: Charlene Panak
Editorial team: Brian Mast & Ruth Hensman

ISBN 13: 978-0-89811-507-9

Printed in the United States of America

You can contact the authors, Bill Moyer or Billy Moyer, at: info@sosleadership.com
View the *SOS Leadership* company and book website at: www.sosleadership.com

We know you will enjoy and benefit from this book from The Leading Edge Publishing Company. Our goal is to provide books and products that give you, the reader, the leading edge in every area of life. For more information on other books and products written and produced to give you the leading edge, go to: www.theleadingedgepublishing.com.

Self-Help / Motivational / Inspirational

Contents

Foreword v

Introduction. vii

Chapter 1: The Assignment. 11

Chapter 2: The Coach 15

Chapter 3: The Teacher. 23

Chapter 4: The Youth Minister 35

Chapter 5: The Final Interview. 45

Chapter 6: The Final Interview: Part Two 63

Chapter 7: The Final Paper. 71

Chapter 8: A New Beginning 77

Epilogue 81

Acknowledgements. 87

About the Authors. 89

Foreword

by Paul J. Meyer

Father and son relationships can be a curious thing. They can be warm and affectionate; cold and distant; insignificant and mundane; and all degrees in between. One thing for sure though is that a man's relationship with his son—and vice versa—will *always* have life-long effects.

While reading *Seeds of Success*, written by the father/son team of Bill and Billy Moyer, I couldn't help but think of my own father, a first generation German immigrant, who taught me some of the hardest-learned—and enduring—lessons of my life. The lessons my father taught me have become the essence of who I am today. Surely, Bill had some equally significant life lessons to share, particularly since he and his son co-wrote it. They didn't let me down. As it turns out, the idea of *significance* is the crux of their story.

It's true we talk a lot about success: becoming successful ... being successful ... living successfully, but as Bill points out, it's not so important that we are successful in our lives, but that we have *significance in our lives*. "I learned the difference between *success* and *significance* ... and I choose significance," he says.

Bill urges us to "plant the seeds ... to live a life of significance by figuring out what matters most. You really do 'Reap what you sow,'" he says. I couldn't agree more.

I am pleased and honored that Bill asked me to write this foreword, not only because we've been friends and business associates for over 20 years, but because I know Bill to be a highly-motivated, inspirational, and spiritual man who truly lives a significant life.

It may be true that the "apple doesn't fall far from the tree," but in the case of Bill, and his son, Billy, I think it's more accurate to say the "seeds of success were planted in the right field and at the right time."

—Paul J. Meyer
New York Times Best-Selling Author & Founder of Success Motivation International, Inc. and 40+ other companies
www.pauljmeyer.com

Introduction

The writing of *Seeds of Success* has been a long time coming. I have spent the past twenty-five years of my life working in companies whose main focus was leadership and developing your full potential. I guess you could say I have had a great deal of success teaching people how to be successful.

But throughout those twenty-five years, my life has changed dramatically. I have developed a deep, personal relationship with God. My faith continues to grow, and I strive to become a man who puts God and family above everything else. Challenging at times, there is a constant battle to overcome my success sickness and workaholic nature. I will be the first to tell you I am not always successful at balancing my priorities. But, I keep trying; I keep stretching. One thing I have learned over the years is that you can never stop growing and developing. There is always something to learn. Maybe that is why I took so long to write this book.

I have spoken at countless business conferences and conventions all over the world, but about eighteen years ago, I began a new ministry. I started speaking to Christian young men and women, as well as their adult leaders. I worked a lot with young people as youth minister of my church. In all the time I spent with youth, I realized their troubles often came from their parents neglecting them. Parents became stressed out, burned out, and worn out from the demands of work, leaving very little left over for their family. In their desire to provide a better life for their kids, they failed to give them what they really wanted—more time with Dad and Mom. This hit hard because I struggled with this early in my life as I climbed the ladder of worldly success.

I took what I learned from the wisdom of these incredible youth and developed a program I would use when speaking to adults. Using the leadership and success principles I learned over the years, I called the program *Seeds of Success*.

The program always went over well, and people constantly told me I should write a book. It was always something I wanted to do as well, but never seemed to be the right time. I was never willing to take away the precious time with my kids while they were home to write a book about spending more time with your family. Nor was I quite sure of what format the book should take.

While developing and presenting the *Seeds of Success* program at workshops, conventions, and retreats, there was always one constant, my youngest son Billy. Usually traveling with me and assisting me at workshops and retreats, he was often my opening speaker. I will always cherish those special times we had together. In fact, he bugged me more than anyone about writing a book.

Finally, after many years of prodding, he finally came to me with an idea. He wanted to co-write the book, and had a plan for how to do it. Everything came together from that point, and the book became a reality.

Seeds of Success is not meant to be a textbook, a traditional business leadership book, or even a book about spirituality. It is really just one man's journey into authentic manhood. Our hope is that in reading this book you will take the stories and life lessons to heart and maybe even develop your own seeds of success.

In my life journey, I have been blessed to study and learn under some of the great Christian Leadership authors in the world. I give special thanks to Dr. John Maxwell, for his leadership in the Christian Church through his many books and programs on Lay Leadership and for our collaboration through Church Growth International.

I also recognize Ken Blanchard and thank him for allowing me to be a part of the early certification process for the Center for Faithwalk Leadership and Lead Like Jesus program.

I especially want to thank Paul J. Meyer, founder of Success Motivation Institute, Leadership Management International, and Church Growth International with whom I have worked. Paul has mentored me for more than twenty years. Most of all, I want to thank God for never giving up on me and loving me unconditionally.

I also want to thank my beautiful wife of thirty years, Rose. She taught me about selfless love as we truly experienced two becoming one. Lastly, I want to thank each of my four children. We are blessed to have very special adult relationships with each of them. It is amazing to see them as spouses, parents, and servants of the Lord. They are a living testimony of what matters most! My successes have been because of them. I also learned the difference between success and significance because of everyone I have thanked, and I choose to live a life of significance!

I hope this book will help you plant the seeds you need to live a life of significance by figuring out what matters most. You really do "Reap what you sow!"

—Bill Moyer

=== 1 ===

The Assignment

With the end of his college career quickly approaching, the student had a lot on his mind. He wondered just what the future would hold for him. Would he meet the woman of his dreams? How would his relationship with his friends be different now? What would he do for a career and, most importantly, how would he be remembered? How could he be successful in his life? He would have to find answers to these questions much sooner than he expected.

It was his final semester and, in one of his classes, a special last assignment was given. The professor stood in front of the class and told them they were to write a final paper that would be much different from every other paper they had written in their school careers.

The paper was to cover the keys to success in business and in life in general. They were advised to go and interview people who had played significant roles in their lives, perhaps a teacher or a good friend. Maybe they could talk to a mentor in their field of study or just anyone who knows about success and is important to them. Ultimately, she said they were to end their interviews by speaking to the one they considered the most successful person they knew, someone who truly impacted their lives.

The thought of this assignment gave the student chills, as it was just what he had been thinking about. He was lost. Enduring four years of college had taken a lot out of him. He constantly wondered if he was good enough, if he mattered to other people. He found it hard to balance priorities, never quite deciding what mattered most to him. Many people "find themselves" at college, but he was still searching. People around him were figuring things out and doing great things, but he was his same old self, which was not quite enough for him.

He, too, wanted to achieve greatness. He longed to be the one who was in love and getting engaged. He desired to have his dream job all lined up and waiting for him. But he did not even know what his dream was; so many had fallen short in the past he was having trouble moving forward. In a rut and needing a change in momentum, this assignment was perfect. It might finally help him define his life purpose.

Knowing just how difficult this assignment would be and thinking more and more about it, he realized it was actually pretty simple. He began thinking about who he could interview, and it became quite obvious who those people were. He had many influential people in his past and present, and they were in a few different areas.

He first thought of a coach who helped him become a better player and, more importantly, a better teammate. Reminiscing about things learned from the coach, he thought back to a season he still considered his hardest ever. He remembered how helpful the coach was and how it paid off in the end. But he would save that for the interview.

Then he thought about a former youth minister who kept him on track in his relationship with God. This man was always around, a great role model for the youth of the church. The student wondered how the minister was able to accomplish all the things he did. So many role models in life let us down, but he never did and that stuck with the student all this time.

And then there was the teacher who changed everything for the student. The one who made him realize he could do anything if he set his mind to it. He knew these three people would have great success stories and might be able to help with the paper.

Then the final person he had to interview came to mind. Supposedly the most successful person he knew, this man truly made a tremendous impact on his life. After only a minute of thinking, it was clear whom he should talk to. He remembered just how much this person did for him, how much he learned about business, life, love, and God from him. He knew this was the one he should talk to.

This was the first time the college student was excited about school work in a long time. Normally an average student who got by because he was naturally smart, he did not spend time reading for classes, doing homework, or even studying for exams. He just went to class and collected his "B's," with an occasional "C." But this assignment was something he could actually learn from. He never thought a person learned from hearing or even seeing; this was his chance to learn by doing something.

More than two thousand years ago Confucius said, **"What I hear I forget. What I see I remember. What I do I understand."**[1]

He knew he would get more from this final paper than he had in his previous four years of school, and he was absolutely right.

---

1. Kung Fu Tzu (Confucius)

$=$ 2 $=$

The Coach

The student contacted his former coach and set up an interview. Armed with a few questions he wanted to ask, he saw the interview as more of a discussion. He really wanted to find out how the coach was able to do what he did, how he defined success, and how he became successful.

The coach met the student at the playground of the old school where they had had numerous practices in the past. As the coach approached, he noticed the student shooting a basketball on the old court. The ball swished through the net, and the coach yelled, "I see you can still shoot."

Embracing the coach with a hug, the student said, "I don't think the shot ever goes away, but I don't think I can move like I used to. I'm much slower now, but, hey, I think I can take anyone in a shooting contest. You know I remember one time you said you could get off your death bed and still make eight-out-of-ten free throws. I think I understand that now. I could get off my death bed and still hit a three-pointer," the student added.

"So what do I owe the pleasure of this visit? You were pretty vague on the phone," the coach asked. The student told the coach the details of the assignment, and they began to talk about their past successes.

There was that one time when the student had been triple teamed in a game, but still managed to lead his team to victory almost single handedly. And the time when a coach of another team advised his players to take the student out because he was too good. The players on that team followed the advice and tackled the student onto the hardwood floor. His chin broke his fall, but left a huge blue-and-purple bump that lasted a week or so. The student considered it a war wound and wore it proudly when he accepted the medal for Most Valuable Player of the tournament.

There were so many memories the two could talk about, but finally the student interrupted and said they needed to discuss the assignment. The coach agreed and told the student to go on and ask whatever he needed to. The student asked, "What are your keys to success, in sports, business, or just life in general?"

"Well that question is one that could take me days to fully answer," replied the coach. "But, as a former coach, how could I talk about success without talking about leadership. Leadership is one of the most important aspects of being successful and with leadership comes a lot of other things. What is the most important position on the court in basketball? I know that's easy for you to answer because you played the position. Of course, it is point guard, and it's important because it is the main position of leadership. People feed off the examples of their leaders, and that's why being a good and effective leader is so important."

The student listened carefully as the coach went on talking. "I cannot keep talking about leadership without talking about a coach that exemplified leadership and success like no other. John Wooden won ten NCAA National Championships by following his own leadership model. I have always shared them with my players. In fact, I shared them with you every year that you played for me. You will remember them all because they are extremely simple. "**Never lie. Never cheat. Never steal. Don't whine. Don't complain. Don't make excuses.**"[2] Those are little things that we all should do every day, and we will be successful. That's not just in basketball or sports, but in our careers and really in our lives."

The student then asked, "So you are telling me that all I have to do to be successful is those six things?"

"No, but it is a great start. You have to have a lot of other things going for you to be successful, but it all starts with leadership and its qualities."

"Well then, if that's the case, what is the most important quality of a leader?" the student asked.

"Now that is the question I was waiting for," replied the coach. "This is one that you should know a lot about. Let me ask you this question first, why did you pick me to interview?"

"I had a lot of success as a player with you. I learned a lot about the game and, now that I think about it, about being a good leader."

"Do you remember any certain event or even a season in which that was true?" the coach questioned.

"The one that most comes to mind was our championship season," the student said.

"Why does that come to mind?"

"That was when I learned about playing as a team."

"Exactly!" the coach exclaimed. "That's what I was hoping you would bring up. That season is still fresh on my mind.

"Let me tell you what I remember from that season," the coach said. "You dominated the competition for several years in a row. You constantly amazed people with your ability on the court, and you just kept getting better. You were young then, and I remember when you would take these long three-point shots and everyone in the crowd would yell NOOO!!! But then it would go in, and they would cheer.

"You had so much talent, but you had yet to learn how to lead a team. You were a scoring point guard. I could tell how much you loved to score, but I always had trouble getting you to distribute the ball. You always thought you could get it done on your own, and as a result we had a few losing years in a row. That was not entirely your fault, as we had little talent on those teams, but I really wanted you to learn how to make a team yours without hogging the ball.

"I got the chance to teach you that lesson in a season where we had more talent than we ever had. By some stroke of luck, we ended up with the two best players in the league, you and Jeff. Unfortunately, you both played the same position and had almost entirely the same game. But he was better then you. You had to learn to be a team player, and that was a really hard thing for you.

"I remember in practice how you would always try to beat Jeff and how, early in the season, you would avoid passing him the ball so you could get your points. The team was faltering because you did not know how to be a leader. But then I decided to switch you and Jeff. I made you the point guard and put the ball in your hands, and I told you something that Hall of Fame coach Dean Smith told Michael Jordan at The University of North Carolina, **'If you can't pass, you can't play.'** I am sure you remember what happened next."

The student said, "I remember like it was yesterday. I began practicing passing at home rather than just shooting. I even began encouraging my teammates on the court and setting an example. I became obsessed with assists. They started being more fun to me than scoring, because it was really the same thing, yet I was helping a teammate score. Then the winning started, which was something I hadn't experienced much of.

"I do remember some hard times though. I would go to school, and my friends would ask me how many points I scored. At times I was ashamed to only say five or six. They didn't understand that ten assists was a good thing. But the more we won, the more I was cured of all that."

"It was an amazing transformation," the coach replied. "It really needed to happen for us to be successful. I have been proud of you a lot over the years I coached you, but never more than that season. Since then I have seen you emerge as a leader in so many other areas, and I like to think I had something to do with that."

"You did, coach," said the student. "That is why I am here talking to you today. I learned so much from you. When I was in high school, I held a lot of leadership positions, none of which would have been possible without what you taught me. I was even president of my junior class and really had to work as a team to accomplish our class goals."

"I love telling and hearing the rest of the story of that season," the coach said. "Do you want to tell it or should I?"

"Go ahead."

"Well, as the season went on, you kept getting better as the team leader, and we just kept winning. We went to the championship game, which was a true test for the team and you as the leader. The team we played was probably better than us. They were certainly bigger. I am pretty sure if we played them ten times they would beat us nine of them. But this game was going to be different.

"Before the game I gave a speech to the team, and I told you all how proud I was of each and every one for reaching this point. I even talked about the movie *Little Giants* and said that, no matter how much bigger and better the other team was, it only takes **ONE** time.

"We went on to play a really good game. Jeff had one of his best games, and you distributed the ball like an old pro. I thought I was watching Pistol Pete Maravich out there. But near the end of the game, it was still close. You had only taken two or three shots the entire game and had only two points. We had the ball and were throwing it in with just seconds left. You were not even looking for the ball when it was thrown at you and knocked you out. You went down right away and had everyone scared.

"After a few seconds, you got up, woozy and hobbled, but you asked to stay in. It was finally your time. You had sacrificed all season for the team, and everyone agreed that it was you who should take the final shot and determine if we would be victorious. Your team-mates had a great deal of respect for you. So I called a play for you. We in-bounded the ball to you, and you went straight for the corner, but were still obviously a little out of it. But you found an opening and five, four, three, two, you put up your shot, one and swish!!! It was a great sound and the perfect way to end the season."

The student then said, "That is still today one of my most thrilling and triumphant moments. I worked so hard that year."

The coach went on to say that teamwork is an essential part of leadership. The people that have that "if-it's-to-be- it's-up-to-me attitude" are the ones that fail in life. With that, the coach passed the ball to the student who instinctively swished a three-point shot.

"Great shot!" exclaimed the coach.

"I couldn't have done it without you," said the student. "We make a great team!"

---

2. Wooden, John. Wooden on Leadership (2005). McGraw Hill Professional. p. 71

SEEDS TO PLANT

Effective leadership is the key to success.

Teamwork—People that try to "go at life alone" are cloaked in failure.

"Never lie. Never cheat. Never steal. Don't whine. Don't complain. Don't make excuses."

Seeds of Success

≡ 3 ≡

The Teacher

The student had gotten what he needed from the coach and really took it to heart. Teamwork was something that was important to him, yet he had forgotten about this great life lesson these last few years. Maybe that was why he was in such a funk during his last semester of college. He wondered if he had tried to go at it alone for too long. It had been a long four years, and he couldn't help but think of all of the group projects he had been a part of in school. He realized he did a lot on his own and rarely worked within the team. He was going to make this a big part of his paper and his plan for his future. He could no longer go at life alone!

He was now ready to move on to the next person on his list, a former teacher. He had a lot of great teachers in his life, but this one just stuck out. This teacher taught him so much about life and was not a traditional classroom teacher. He arranged to meet the teacher at a local bookstore.

Walking into the bookstore, the student spotted his teacher right where he knew he would be, sitting by the window reading a book. He quickly went up to the teacher, gave him a hug, and sat down. Having already explained the assignment, they immediately began the interview.

The student quickly got to the point by asking, "What made you successful? What would you say has been the key to your success as a teacher?"

The teacher thought for a moment, and then responded, "I have been successful teaching because I am always prepared; but, I think you are really asking me what the key to a successful life is, right?"

"I guess that is what I am asking," the student replied.

"Well, my life has been about teaching and helping other people, but in order to do that I first had to be able to help myself. A great teacher is a mentor and most of all a leader. And leadership is really just influence. So I had to be a good example for my students and for everyone around me. In order for me to do that, I had to first overcome some bad influences I had. Did I ever tell you why I teach eighth grade?"

"I think I remember you talking about it, but why don't you refresh my memory," the student said.

"I had one of my most inspirational teachers in eighth grade," the teacher went on. "It was actually in a Sunday school class much like the one I teach now. I was starting to really get into church and learning about God and the Bible at that time. My eighth grade teacher was the reason I became so gung-ho. When he talked, it was like God was talking directly through him. He quickly became my Christian role model. I was always the class clown who disrupted the class, but in his class I always listened attentively and never acted up. That first semester was, at that time, the high point of my spirituality, and it was because of that teacher."

"So this teacher was a positive influence on you?" the student asked.

"That was the case during the first semester," he continued. "We had a break from class for Christmas and, when I came back for the first class after the break, my teacher was not there. We had a substitute, and I asked where our teacher was. The substitute said he did not know. The next week another substitute showed up, and I began to get aggravated. I asked again where our teacher was, and I still got no answers. The next week the same thing happened, but this time I was told he would not be coming back. I wanted to know why so I took matters into my own hands.

"The teacher had a daughter that went to my school, so I found her one day and asked her why her dad wasn't my teacher anymore. She looked at me with sadness and began to cry. She told me that over the Christmas break her dad left his family and moved in with his twenty-three-year-old secretary.

"This was a huge shock to me. How could this teacher, who was the perfect example of a Christian man and spoke the word of God to me so powerfully, do something like that? This was the man I was trying to be like? I decided that day that if being a Christian meant doing things like that, then I did not want any part of it. I didn't go to church again for twenty years except to get married and for a few funerals. That is the power of negative influences."

The teacher looked at the student and asked, "You mentioned before about how you were in a funk in your life and were not sure what to do next. Do you know why that is?"

The student answered, "After hearing your story, I am starting to think some negative influences have been one of the reasons."

"Is there any negative influence in particular?" the teacher questioned.

"There is one that came to my mind when you were telling your story," the student replied. "In my third year of college, I had a relationship with someone who was not a good influence on me. In fact, I let the relationship take over my life, which meant my whole life was negative.

"The summer before my junior year I met a girl who dramatically altered my life. Unfortunately, it was for the worse. I immediately fell for this girl and, in the beginning, things seemed great. But as time went on, I began committing myself completely to her, but she never committed herself to me. The entire relationship was about me trying to make her realize her feelings for me.

"In doing that, I neglected the people I cared about and who actually cared about me—my family and close friends. The friends I met the previous year became mere acquaintances because she dominated my life. I was okay with all of this at the time because I was in love with her. Eventually, she broke my heart and completely cut me out of her life. I was so devastated.

"It was not until a few months later I finally realized how negative the relationship was for me. I realized how much this girl took advantage of me and, because of that, I spent all my energy on her and my life suffered. I became an angry and depressed person, who no one wanted to be around. The few people that did, I avoided. I had the two worst semesters in college as far as grades were concerned. Because of her negative influence on me, I had a lot to make up for in my other relationships, and I am still working on that now more than a year later.

"I think that is one of the main reasons I am in this funk. I have been trying to rid myself of this negativity and focus on my goals, but I am not even sure what my goals are anymore."

"It sounds like I don't have to explain the power of negative influence to you," the teacher said. "But hearing that story and about the state you have been in lately makes me think of something I received in an email a few weeks ago. I think I could tell you a few more stories and some more keys to success, but sometimes it is better to send you somewhere else to find the answers. I will forward you the email and you can watch the video that it links to. I think that might give you a little perspective. After you watch it, give me a call and we can talk about it." The student agreed, and they parted ways.

The next day the student opened the email he received from the teacher. It contained a link to a video and a brief note from the teacher that read, "Maybe this will help you remember your childhood dreams and that those negative influences we talked about can make you stronger. Watch this video. It will be the greatest lesson I have ever taught you, even though it is from the mouth of someone else."

The video was called *The Last Lecture*. A tradition for some college professors, they give a lecture as if it was the last one they would ever give. The student thought this sounded cool at first, although he was a little annoyed at the idea of watching a lecture considering he had been doing that for the past four years. But he watched anyway and was not disappointed.

Early in the lecture he realized the lecturer, a professor at Carnegie Mellon University named Randy Pausch, was actually giving his last lecture. Not because of the tradition, but because he had been diagnosed with pancreatic cancer and had only months to live. After hearing this, the student began to listen more attentively. This dying man, who was about to leave three young kids and a wife, was more upbeat about life than was the student.

Pausch talked about achieving childhood dreams. He told of wanting to become a Walt Disney Imagineer, which he ended up doing, and of wanting to play in the National Football League, a dream that did not come true, but from which he learned a lot. Pausch stated, **"Experience is what you get when you don't get what you want."**[3] He went on to say that, **"Brick walls are there for a reason; they let us prove how badly we want something."**[4]

"Experience is what you get, when you don't get what you want."

"Brick walls are there for a reason; they let us prove how badly we want something."

"We cannot change the cards we are dealt, just how we play the hand."

Quotes from Randy Pausch, The Last Lecture (2008)

At the end of this lecture the student found himself in tears. He could not believe how on fire this man was about his life, even though he had been dealt a bad hand. Here the student was moping and stressing about little things and neglecting his own dreams. This guy was achieving his against all the odds.

The student called the teacher and got his voice-mail. Leaving a message he said, "I want to thank you for meeting with me and for everything you have done for me over the years. I especially want to thank you for the gift of *The Last Lecture*. I have heard so many people talk about a singular moment when everything changes for them, and I believe I have now had mine. I had my 'ah-ha moment.' I am now ready to start living my life and achieving my dreams."

Thanking the teacher one more time, the student ended with his favorite quote from *The Last Lecture*, **"We cannot change the cards we are dealt, just how we play the hand."**[5]

"It's about time I started playing my hand," he said.

The teacher returned the student's call shortly after he received the message. He was glad the student enjoyed the video, as he knew he would. He then provided the student with one final example of how to be successful. It was something simple but vital, according to the teacher.

"At the beginning of your message to me," he said, "you thanked me for meeting with you and passing along the video; that is one of my keys to success. In fact, I think it is the most important—gratitude. When I look back on my life I realize how many people have helped me get to where I am. I am so grateful to everyone who has been a part of my success. The success I achieved is also their success.

"But just being grateful is not enough. You must show gratitude! This can simply be done by saying thank you in a voicemail, as you did with me. It could be a thank you note or anything really. Let me tell you about perhaps the greatest thank you I have received.

"I used to substitute at a local high school every so often. I knew all of the students pretty well. I took a liking to one young man. He was a gifted athlete and extremely bright. On top of that, he was one of the nicest guys I had ever met. But this big, strong, young athlete was dealt a tough hand one year, much like Randy Pausch. He was diagnosed with Leukemia. He fought and got better, but then got worse.

"Whenever I was at the school, I would go to his locker and slip a little note in it. It was usually a card with an inspirational quote or a Bible verse. I never put my name on it, so I never thought he knew it was me leaving them.

"One day I was at the school teaching a class. The young man had just gone through a tough few weeks. He was able to come to school, but not allowed to go to class because he was susceptible to other students' illnesses. I taught a really good class, but was sad he was unable to hear it.

"Later that day as I was walking down the hall, I heard a whisper and there he was. He was in a small room with a little window. Opening the door, he asked me what I was doing there. I told him I just got finished teaching a class and was sorry he missed it. Then he asked me if I would stay and teach it to him. I did what he asked, and he seemed grateful to interact with someone. This was all the gratitude I needed, but I received more at the end of our conversation.

"As I was leaving he told me he wanted to thank me for something. Then he pulled out of his pocket a big stack of notes. They were all the little notes I had left him over the past months. He told me he knew it was me and that they always brightened his day, inspiring him to keep fighting. The young man lost his battle with cancer, but not before playing out his hand completely.

"His gratitude for something simple that I had done helped me become a better teacher and a better leader. He was able to show gratitude in the worst of times. Since then I have been quick to thank everyone who has helped me, no matter how big or small. Thank you is a powerful phrase that can never be overused. I believe it is not used enough. The people who are truly successful know how important gratitude is, and they show it all the time."

The student was touched by the story, and began thinking about all the people who had helped him over the years. Wondering if he had shown enough gratitude, he decided right then and there he would show more gratitude with people. He also decided to make a list of people who helped him in the past; he would write letters to them expressing his appreciation for all they had done. He told this to the teacher, and the teacher agreed it was a good idea. The interview was now over and the student, knowing that "thank you" could never be overused, again thanked his former teacher for his help in the interview and in his life.

---

3. Pausch, Randy. The Last Lecture (2008). Hyperion Books
4. Pausch, Randy. The Last Lecture (2008). Hyperion Books
5. Pausch, Randy. The Last Lecture (2008). Hyperion Books.

SEEDS TO PLANT

Leadership is influence—
Set a good example!

Negative influences will bring you down if you let them.

Follow your dreams—"We cannot change the cards we are dealt, just how we play the hand."

Show Gratitude! A simple thank you goes a long way.

Seeds of Success

4

The Youth Minister

After meeting with his former teacher and watching *The Last Lecture*, the student was now on fire and ready to move quickly on his final paper. He already had two great interview experiences and was feeling much better about the assignment and, most importantly, about his life.

For his next interview, the student called his former youth minister. This man with his wife had spent fourteen years as youth minister at the student's church. Growing up, the student was fortunate enough to spend a lot of time with the youth group, even before he was old enough to be in it. In high school he became extremely active because of the model this man set.

The student met the youth minister at their church and, unlike the other interviews, he began immediately. Having already explained the assignment, he asked him,

"What are your keys to success? How were you able to become such a good leader?"

The youth minister responded, "The most important part of my success as a youth minister has been to realize that people, especially kids, become like their leader."

"Leadership is influence," replied the student.

"Exactly," the youth minister said. "It was always important to me to be a good role model for the kids I worked with because I knew some of them did not have good role models at home. I wanted to model for them what a good marriage looks like and what a good parent does. I have seen a lot of bad parents throughout my life and many bad role models. I know the terrible effect it can have on a person.

"Parents are often too concerned with their children being the best at everything. Whether it is school, music, acting, or sports, parents are either not involved at all or are sometimes too involved. One of the biggest mistakes parents and other adults make is this—they do not realize **kids are entrusted to us for God's glory. They are not for our glory**.

"Years ago I coached a little league baseball team, and one of the kids dropped a fly ball in right field. That drop cost us the game. After the game the kid's father screamed at him and punched him in the chest. I remember he shouted at him, 'How could you embarrass me like that?'

"I never wanted to be that type of father or the type of leader who lives his life through the kids. So, as a youth minister, I made it my mission to set a good example not only for the kids, but for their parents as well. Everyone needs positive influences in their life, but unfortunately the negative influences are the ones we focus on."

"It's funny you say that," the student said. "I was just talking about negative influences with someone else, and I am planning on making it a big part of my paper. But I hadn't thought of talking about positive influences. It's almost like a natural human instinct to think about the negative first."

The youth minister agreed with the student and asked him to talk about a positive influence. The student began, "One of the most positive relationships was with a friend beginning in my senior year of high school and continuing on over the following years. I taught a Sunday school class at church; I'm sure you remember that. One of the students in the class seemed to take a liking to me. I spoke to her quite a bit before and after class and then she joined the youth group. We saw a lot of each other.

Kids are entrusted to us for God's glory. They are not for our glory.

"In the fall she asked me to be her Confirmation sponsor, and a great friendship began. The greatest part of our friendship was that I was able to mentor her through some tough times. She was going through some parts of her life that I had already been through. I was able to help her avoid some of the mistakes I made. I would say I was a positive influence on her life. But the amazing thing about this friendship was that, although I was the older and supposedly wiser person, she helped me as much, if not more, than I helped her. I was at a crossroads in my life and was searching for something, almost like I am now. She helped me realize what I needed most was church. She did this by asking me to be her sponsor and by giving me a reason to help out with the youth group, even though I had already graduated."

The youth minister enjoyed the student's story and agreed that more focus is put on the negative. He told the student he should discuss both positive and negative influences in his paper. He then told the student he may have underestimated the influence he had on his friend, and he should never forget that.

The student then said, "Any impact I had on her life was a direct result of you. You said people become like their leaders and the reason I told you that story was to show you the impact I was able to have on someone else because of you." The youth minister thanked the student for his kind words.

Then the youth minister switched gears to another important characteristic of leaders and a key to success. "I think the next part I am going to talk about is extremely important for us as servants. Stewardship, I believe, is a vital aspect of leadership and people who are successful. I'm sure you have heard the old expression, 'to whom much is given, much is expected.' That statement is talking about stewardship.

Jesus talked about stewardship often throughout his life. He did so specifically in one parable that I think you will know. Why don't you open up the Bible over there to Matthew 25:14-30 and read about the parable of the talents."

The student opened the Bible and began to read aloud.

"Again, it will be like a man going on a journey called his servants and entrusted his possessions to them. To one he gave five talents; to another, two; to a third, one-to each according to his ability. Then he went away. Immediately the one who received five talents went and traded with them, and made another five. Likewise, the one who received two made another two. But the man who had received one went off and dug a hole in the ground and buried his master's money.

"After a long time the master of those servants came back and settled accounts with them. The one who had received five talents came forward bringing the additional five. He said, 'Master, you gave me five talents. See, I have made five more.' His master said to him, 'Well done, my good and faithful servant. Since you were faithful in small matters, I will give you great responsibilities. Come, share your master's joy.'

"[Then] the one who had received two talents also came forward and said, 'Master, you gave me two talents. See, I have made two more.' His master said to him, 'Well done, my good and faithful servant. Since you were faithful in small matters, I will give you great responsibilities. Come, share your master's joy.'

"Then the man who had received the one talent came forward and said, 'Master, I knew you were a demanding person, harvesting where you did not plant and gathering where you did not scatter; so out of fear I went off and buried your talent in the ground. Here it is back.' His master said to him in reply, 'You wicked, lazy servant! So you knew that I harvest where I did not plant and gather where I did not scatter? Should you not then have put my money in the bank so that I could have got it back with interest on my return?

"Now then! Take the talent from him and give it to the one with ten. For to everyone who has, more will be given and he will grow rich; but from the one who has not, even what he has will be taken away. And throw this useless servant into the darkness outside, where there will be wailing and grinding of teeth.'"[6]

After the student was finished, the youth minister then said, "Now it would be easy for you or anyone for that matter to think that stewardship is just about donating money to the church or to people in need. Giving of your treasures is a part of it, but it is not the most important. The parable talked about 'talents,' which was money in those days, but a 'talent' also, represents two other things Jesus asks us to give. He asks us to give of our time, talents, and treasures. Notice how he left treasures for the end. Stewardship is about being a good steward of your other gifts God has given you. If God has given you a special gift, a certain talent, or ability, you are supposed to use it to serve him. If He gave it to you, He did so for a reason."

The student understood just what the youth minister was talking about. He had been given so many gifts, but he did not always use them to serve God or to serve other people. He sometimes thought he should focus on his career and making money and give away a portion of that abundance.

Then the youth minister asked him what he did to serve God and others. He answered, "Well, I have been busy lately so I have not been able to do as much as I wanted to, but I have gone to this homeless breakfast a few times and, of course, I go to Mass every week as well, but I am not involved in church like I used to be.

The youth minister then said, "I'm sad to hear you are not as involved anymore. A few years ago, when you helped out with the youth group, you were such a positive role model. I also remember how great a lector you were at Mass.

"You know the way you answered my question made me think of something my former priest said to me years ago. I was at the church late and noticed a light on as I was leaving. When I went in, I saw our priest mopping the floor. I said, 'Father, why are you mopping the floor?' He told me he usually did it because they did not have anyone else to. I told him I would do it, but he refused. He said, 'Mopping the floor is not the greatest gift that you have. You have other gifts to use and I would appreciate it if you would use perhaps your greatest gift, your big mouth, to find someone to mop the floor for me.'

"He meant that as a compliment. He was right. Mopping the floor was not a gift of mine. I was given the gift of being able to talk to people and in front of large numbers of people. I was also given the gift of being able to work with youth. I have been using those gifts to serve God for many years now and that is why I have been so blessed or successful as they call it in the secular world. And by the way, I did find someone to mop the floor for him."

That wrapped up the interview and, after the youth minister left, the student began to think about everything they discussed. He thought about his life and how he did not spend enough time serving others and being a good steward of the many gifts God had given him. He decided he would begin to try and use all the gifts he had been given to multiply God's kingdom rather than bury them in the ground.

Then he reflected on all the positive people in his life. He had talked so much with the youth minister about positive influences he wanted to be more positive in his own life. He thought about his mother and brothers and sister. He thought about the relationship he had with his best friend whom he had known for eighteen years. He even thought back on the negative relationship he had talked about with his teacher and was able to find some positives in that. He realized that, yes, negative thinking and influences have great power. **But there is no greater power than positive thinking!**

---

6. Excerpt from Matthew 25:14-30 in the New American Bible

SEEDS TO PLANT

Leadership is influence—Be a good role model for your kids!

The power of positive influences and thinking outweighs the negative.

Be a steward for the Lord. Share your time, talents, and treasures with the world willingly and lovingly.

Serve God by using the gifts He gave you.

Seeds of Success

═ 5 ═

The Final Interview

The student was now ready for his final interview. This would be the longest and most intense interview yet, but he would not be disappointed. He was all set to meet the man whom he called the most successful person he knew. The man who had most influenced his life. He had learned so much about how to live from him and was truly excited to learn more.

The student met Bob at his home, which was quite modest for a man who realized so much success throughout his life. He went into Bob's home office and wasn't surprised when he did not see any awards hanging on the wall. He only saw pictures of Bob's family.

As they sat down Bob started the discussion off by asking the student what he had learned so far in his interviews. The student spoke about leadership and how it starts with teamwork. He also talked about positive and negative influences and how people become like their leaders.

Then Bob said, "It seems like you have gotten some pretty good information already, but I think I can add some things and perhaps allow you to interpret the word 'success' differently. Before I get into all of that though, I want to know what you think success is and how you believe you can achieve it."

The student answered, "Success to me is really all about goal setting. I have always believed you can have anything you want or be anything you want as long as you set a clear goal and you work hard enough to achieve it. I have three simple steps I follow when trying to achieve a goal. They are in the form of quotes by three of my heroes.

"First, Tug McGraw[7] said, 'Ya gotta believe!' Before you can work towards a goal, you must first believe in yourself and believe that it is possible. Second, Rocky Balboa[8] said, 'Go for it!' Once you believe something is possible, you have to take the risk and make it happen. Lastly, Jim Valvano[9] said, 'Don't give up. Don't ever give up.' Doing those first two is not enough. You have to keep doing them over and over. You have to keep working as hard as you can until you achieve your goal."

Bob thought for a minute and then said, "You sound exactly like me when I was your age. I must say that I agree with your assessment of how to achieve goals. I have seen a lot of different diagrams and charts on goal setting and achieving and I believe those three quotes work better than anything I have ever seen. If you want to have success in business than you should approach it exactly how you described, but I want to make this one point very clear. If you use that approach in your life, you will end up being extremely disappointed, and I guarantee you will never find success, at least the type of success that I believe is important."

The student was a little turned off by this statement and Bob, in seeing this, explained what he was talking about a little more. "When I said that you sounded exactly like me when I was your age, well I meant that truthfully. To be completely honest I sounded like that into my thirty's. I want to tell you when that changed for me."

The student urged Bob to go on and he did. "I have always been a hard worker. I have a disease that a lot of people in America suffer from; it's called being a workaholic. About twenty-three years ago, I started my own business. It was a franchise of a bigger company based in Texas. I worked extremely hard in this business and pretty much used your model of how to be successful.

"I started becoming successful in the business, but I was working a lot. I had three kids at this point. One year I attended the parent company's world convention, and I saw all the awards that were given and I set a goal that I would get one of biggest awards the next year. So I approached that goal as you said you approach them.

"I worked eighteen hours a day, sometimes more, and had little time for my family. I really did not have anything else in my life besides work and family, and work always came first. I justified it like many people do, by saying I was doing it for my family. The truth was I was doing it for myself.

"By the time the next convention rolled around, I had achieved my goal. I was going to be honored with the second highest award. I was not eligible for the highest one. So I went to the convention, and was really excited for the awards ceremony. I was even more excited for the after-party that only award winners were invited to. It was in the suite on the top floor of the hotel, where you could get to only if you had a special gold key.

"The awards ceremony began, and I sat in anticipation for my award. I had written this awesome speech and could not wait to speak. My speech said you can have anything you want, do anything you want, be anything you want as long as you are willing to pay the price. Does that sound familiar?"

The student nodded because this was almost the exact phrase he had used when talking about success. Bob went on.

"It was almost my turn to go on stage when the emcee made a mistake. He announced the winner of the highest award before me. The man who won this was someone whom I knew and whom everyone in the company knew. He got to the microphone, and I was stunned with what he said. He talked about how most people in the audience knew that this was a very tough year for him. Although he had his best year ever in his business, he had his worst year ever in his personal life. His young six-year-old son had died of leukemia. He talked about how blessed he was to have had those six years and how thankful he was for all of the family and friends who were so supportive during this difficult time. He shared with us that 'what matters most' in life is your love of God and the special time you have with your family. He challenged us to not miss those precious moments.

"Hearing this man talk had left me numb, so when my big moment finally came, when they called my name and invited me to the stage to accept the award I had sacrificed almost everything to attain, I was speechless for one of the few times in my life. I forgot all about my speech and just whispered thank you and sat down.

"After the event, I was in a fog as people crowded around me to congratulate me and have their picture taken with me and my trophy to use for their visualization board for next year's goals. This magical moment I had dreamed about was somehow shallow and empty. Later, I used my gold key to go to the prestigious reception for award winners. As the door to the suite opened, I looked inside and saw all of my role models in business. It was just as I imagined it would be, but it felt empty and meaningless. I closed the door and left the party; I just went for a walk alone.

"On that walk I had a conversation with myself. I just could not understand why I was unhappy after I had just achieved the goal I had been killing myself to achieve. 'Why am I never satisfied? Why, whenever I finally get what I want is it not enough?' I was suffering from severe disappointment.

"Disappointment is usually the result of unmet expectations. The more unrealistic the expectations, the greater your disappointment will be. But, I had exceeded my expectations! 'What is wrong with me, I thought?'

"As I walked in the middle of the night in this city, I began to hear footsteps. I looked over my shoulder and noticed a man following me. I walked faster; he walked faster. I slowed down; he slowed down. My street instincts told me I was in danger. No one was around, and no buildings were in sight. I had walked quite a distance from my hotel. My pulse was racing, and I glanced back again and thought, 'I am too slow and out of shape to run, so I will have to confront him.'

"I finally turned around quickly and confronted him by yelling, 'WHAT DO YOU WANT?' He jumped about two feet in the air. I almost scared him to death.

"He then said in a soft voice, 'You look like you could use someone to talk to. I thought maybe I could get us some coffee, and we could talk.'

"He was a homeless man and I was skeptical, but I gave him two dollars, and he walked away promising to return soon with the coffee. I did not expect to see him again. I was sure he would take my money to buy drugs or booze. I hurriedly began walking back to my hotel, thankful to be alive and only out two bucks.

"About ten minutes later, as I could see my hotel in the distance, he came running up to me, breathless but with two cups of coffee in his hands. We sat under a tree near the hotel on two lounge chairs from the pool. I am not sure why, but I poured out my heart to this man. I told him about the award and about how I was so disappointed. Then I told him about my childhood and about my dad being an abusive alcoholic. I talked about a bad experience I had with the church and another one with a poor leader who disappointed me. I told him how lucky I was to have a great wife and amazing kids but that even after having everything I wanted, I was still empty inside.

"After hearing all I had to say, this homeless man told me it was clear to him what I was missing in my life—a personal relationship with God. He told me God was calling me home to Him and all I needed to do was accept his invitation. Then he told me his story.

"He had been living a comfortable, middle-class life when he got laid off from his job. He had no savings and his bills began to mount up. He began drinking all night and sleeping all day. His wife left him and took the kids. Losing his house and his family, had been on the streets for almost three years, having no contact with his family for two years. I told him it was time for him to go home, too. I helped him call his family and was with him a few hours later when his wife picked him up to take him home.

"Now it was my turn to go home, back to the loving arms of a forgiving God. I went home and told my wife about what happened and that God was calling me back to the church. She had been praying for this for the ten years we were married, and this was an answer to her faithful prayers.

"I began a period of study and reflection in the Catholic Church called RCIA (Rite of Christian Initiation for Adults). A little over a year after meeting God's messenger in a deserted field a long way from home, I stood at the altar of our church and, with my wife as my sponsor, received the precious body and blood of Jesus Christ for the first time, and became a Catholic.

"The year I won that award was the most successful business year I have ever had, but it was also the worst year as well. I worked and worked, but I missed out on family events and on time with my kids. I now know that year was not a successful one at all, but since then all my years have been successful, but not because of what I have done in my career."

"That is a pretty intense story," the student said. "It seems to me you are saying that being successful has little to do with one's career or personal accolades?"

"It really doesn't have anything to do with those things," Bob said. "This is my opinion of course, but it is one I have developed over the years. I always tell people that in order to be successful in life they must first plant the seeds of success. Some of those seeds you have talked about already in your other interviews, but I am going to add to them.

"One of the most important seeds of success is forgiveness. People in this world too often hold grudges against other people. Jesus preached about forgiveness all the time. He was able to forgive the people who crucified him as he was hanging on the cross and moments away from death. My forgiveness story begins right after the story I just told you."

The student asked Bob to tell him the story as he was extremely intrigued about where this interview was going. Bob began telling the story.

"One of the reasons I was so unhappy with my life at that time was because of how difficult of a childhood I had. I told you I grew up in a home with an abusive alcoholic for a father. I spent a lot of years hating him. Something I left out in the last story was how at the end of my conversation with the homeless man I looked into his eyes and saw my dad. I was unsure of what that meant, but I went home on fire to join the church. As I said, I began the process to join the church by joining RCIA.

"A couple weeks before I was supposed to come into the church the group had a retreat, and I was asked to share my story. I told the story and also talked about the negative effect my dad had on me. After the retreat, the deacon came up to me and advised me to not come into the church because he felt I was not ready. He could tell I still had all of this bitterness built up towards my dad. He told me I would never be fully ready until I forgave him.

"I thought a lot about this and decided I would forgive him. I went to see him and told him about everything that was going on in my life and the pain I was feeling because of him. But after all of that, I told him I loved him and that I forgave him for everything. He began to cry and then a funny thing happened.

"I began to remember the good things that happened that were buried under the bitterness. I remembered him sitting by my bedside after coming home from a long day and night of working. I remembered him talking to me when I was sleeping, telling me how proud he was of me. Forgiving him changed my life and allowed me to see him much differently. It changed my past and my future; it also allowed me to become a better father. But that's not all it did.

"Forgiveness is an unbelievable thing. By forgiving him, I not only changed my life, but I changed his life as well. He quit drinking and began to be a more loving husband. A few years later my mother had a stroke, and he had to do everything for her. He carried her to the bathroom and bathed her. He fed her and, most importantly, he loved and nurtured her. This was a woman who had spent over forty years in a difficult marriage filled with anger, bitterness, and abuse, but in the end she felt loved. By forgiving him, I changed her life.

"After she died, my dad began to have a much closer relationship with his grandchildren and none of them know the man that I knew as a child. They knew their grandfather as a kind, sweet, and loving man, and that is exactly how it should be. So my forgiveness also changed my kid's lives because they got to have that special bond with their grandfather."

"I had no idea forgiveness was so powerful," the student said. "It makes me think of all the times I have not forgiven people. I wonder if I would be different if I would have forgiven them or maybe if they would be different."

"It is never too late to forgive," Bob said.

The student then asked Bob what the next seed of success was. "The seeds do not always have to be in a certain order, but this next one goes hand-in-hand with forgiveness. In order to become an effective leader and lead a successful life, one must first overcome one's past. **Becoming requires overcoming**."

"This is something that I had to do because of the way I grew up," Bob said. "You were telling me earlier about the teacher you interviewed and how he taught eigth grade because of the negative influence of his teacher. That is overcoming the past. Maybe a person has to overcome a negative childhood or poor parents. Sometimes people have to overcome addictions. Some people have to overcome one bad decision or a moment in their life that did not go their way. Do you understand what I am saying?"

"Yes, and now that you mention it, I have some firsthand experience with overcoming the past," the student said. Bob asked the student to tell him about it.

"When I was growing up, I had a lot of goals and dreams. One of my biggest dreams was to go to Temple University. It was in Philadelphia, which was my favorite place in the world. Everyone knew that was where I wanted to go. But then I got the letter that would forever alter my life. 'We regret to inform you that your application to Temple University has been denied.'

"It was one of the worst feelings I ever felt. I wasn't used to failing. I have lived with the disappointment of that letter for the past four years. I actually think that is one of the reasons I have been in such a rut lately. I still keep wondering, what if? How would my life be different? But when I think about it, I realize I would have missed out on a lot if that letter would have been different. I think I have become who I am today because of that letter. I still believe I am overcoming it, but I am better for it."

"That is a pretty good example of overcoming. Why do you think you have been able to overcome this?" Bob asked.

"To be completely honest, it has gotten easier and easier over the past four years because I am not the same person I was back then. I have changed," the student said.

"I was hoping you would say something about change. Change is also an extremely important part of leadership and of being successful. My dad changed after I forgave him. I changed when I got my award. People are constantly changing, but the important thing about change is accepting it. Before a person can accept change they must have insight. **Insight precedes change**. Let me give you an example of that.

"As I was trying to rework my life years ago, I started tracking my goals. Tracking is an important part of goal setting. I set a goal to spend fifteen minutes one-on-one with my kids each day and used a tracking sheet to check it off. After a month, three out of my four kids had thirty checks, but one only had four checks. I did not even realize how I had neglected him until the end of the month. But it was not just the tracking sheet that made me realize my mistake.

"One day my son told me he wanted to show me a fort he had built. He was so excited about it, but I didn't have time to see it. I told him I would look later. He waited and waited. When I finally got home from work, I had forgotten all about it. I walked into the room and saw he had destroyed the fort. Not only did I not spend fifteen minutes with him a day like I did with the other kids, but I did not even have time to take one minute to look at what my son had built.

"At that moment I knew I needed to change. I had gained valuable insight and thankfully I listened. I changed and reworked my priorities. If I would not have done this, it could have dramatically changed his life in a negative way. So my advice to you is to never be afraid to change because **if you do what you've always done, you will _be_ what you've always been.**"

The student was so surprised at this story because, although he knew Bob quite well, he had never known him in the way he portrayed himself in that story, or any of the stories for that matter. The student then began to think about change.

"All of this talk about change makes me think of something else I have had to work to overcome. I realized while you were talking that I fear change. This project has been great so far in many ways, and one of the main ones is that it has made me think about the reasons I am so scared about graduating. If I really think about it, I am really just scared of change."

"At your age, being afraid of change is normal," Bob said. "You have a lot of new things coming into your life and a lot of changes happening around you. I think the last thing I said is something you should really take to heart, so I will say it again. **If you do what you've always done, you will _be_ what you've always been.**"

Bob said he thought they should get into some more of the seeds of success, so they moved on in their discussion.

"Humility is another important seed that you must plant in order to be successful. I have people ask me all the time what they need to do to be a better leader. Humility is always something I stress to them. Humility is one of the hardest things to do for a human, especially for me to do as a man. We have been taught to strive and to achieve. We have been trained to stand up and say, 'Look at me. I did it. Look how big my trophy is.' We must be confident, but that tends to lead to arrogance, which is a brick wall to success.

If you do what you've always done, you will be what you've always been.

"When I think of humility, I always think of Matthew 23:11 in the Bible. It says, 'The greatest among you must be your servant.'[10] Serving others is one way to remain humble. Jesus washed the feet of his apostles to show them that he was their servant. We are on this earth to serve one another and that is something you should never forget."

The student said that humility had always been tough for him, but he was constantly working on being better. He asked Bob to continue on with another seed.

"Accountability is also an important part of success," Bob said. "Humility and serving others are important, but accountability is also a must. We must be willing to live an examined life, to give others permission to call us out when we get off track. This is much like your story with your coach calling you out on your lack of assists and holding you accountable to change your game. Gratitude, which I believe you have already discussed, is also important.

"Accountability is really just putting yourself out there. It is really 'going for it' as you said earlier. Everyone needs someone to hold them accountable at work, but in life you must also hold yourself accountable.

"Let me ask you a question. Being a college student, you must know a little about the economy. What would our economy be like if every manager in America held their people accountable for what they are paid to do? How would productivity look? What would your own life look like if you held yourself accountable for your actions?

"When people are held accountable they either step up or they step out. But a person cannot stay stepped out for long. At some point they have to move on or step up. If not, they will never experience growth.

"Let me give you an example. I'm sure you have worked on several group projects in school. Everyone in the group does exactly what they committed to do but one team member doesn't do anything. You confront that person and hold them accountable for what they committed to do. They now are forced to make a choice. They can either step up and complete their part of the project or step out of the way and allow the rest of the team to complete it or to replace them with someone else. Eventually, if that person steps out, they will reach a choice point in their lives. They must step up and do what is necessary to complete their goals or move on from the goals and find something different to commit to."

"I understand exactly what you are saying about being held accountable," the student said. "I have been in a few groups where I have had to hold team members accountable and unfortunately some people have chosen to step out. For me personally, my best grades have been when I set goals for a class and hold myself accountable when I get grades back. When I see I am not doing as good as I could be doing, I step up and do better. Regrettably, I think I have often stepped out when it comes to being accountable in my life. That is something I need to change."

"It is good you understand that it must change," Bob said. "That means you are already holding yourself accountable."

"I am going to tell you another quick story and then I think we may have to continue this tomorrow, we have been talking for over three hours," Bob said.

"I had a good friend who loved to play golf. He always wanted me to play golf with him, but after all the struggles I had with priorities—some of which I have yet to even tell you—I always turned him down. You see, playing golf was great, but it meant I would lose that time with my kids and my wife. I was not willing to do that anymore.

"A few years later, that friend of mine got cancer. As I was sitting with him one day, just a few days before he died, he said something to me that I will always remember. He said, 'If I knew this was going to happen, I would have played a lot less golf and spent more time with my family.'"

This story hit the student pretty hard and he began to think about his definition of success. He had always had that attitude that he could do anything he wanted or be anything he wanted, as long as he was willing to pay the price. But what price would he have to pay?

Bob and the student concluded the interview, but there was still more they needed to talk about. They agreed to talk the next day. The student had gained a lot from this part of the interview, but the best was yet to come.

[7.] Frank Edwin "Tug" McGraw, a standout relief pitcher with the Mets and the Philadelphia Phillies, is best known for his antics on and off the field and for getting the final out in the 1980 World Series for the Phillies. He passed away from cancer in 2004.

[8.] Rocky Balboa is a fictional character played by Sylvester Stallone in the *Rocky* Movie Series.

[9.] Jim Valvano coached the North Carolina State basketball team to an NCAA National Championship in 1983. He was later diagnosed with cancer and died in 1993.

[10.] Matthew 23:11 in the New American Bible

SEEDS TO PLANT

Forgiveness will change your life and others lives as well.

Becoming requires Overcoming!

Don't be afraid of Change! If you do what you've always done, you will be what you've always been.

Be God's humble servant! Arrogance is a brick wall to success.

Be accountable. Step up or Step out!

Seeds of Success

$=\ 6\ =$

The Final Interview: Part Two

The next day, they again met at Bob's house, and began part two of the interview right away. This would be a shorter talk, but the student would learn everything he needed to know. The interviews he had done already would all come together with what Bob had to say.

The student said to Bob, "Let's go ahead and get started. I barely slept last night thinking about all we talked about, but I have a feeling you have a few more important insights for me."

"Indeed, I do," Bob said. "In fact, everything we have covered so far has been leading up to what I am going to tell you now. You wanted to know what the keys to success were, and I have told you about some seeds you can plant. But, if you only get one thing from this interview, get this. The seeds of success I have been talking about and even the ones you have heard about in the other interviews are not about finding success at all.

"The last story I told you yesterday was about my friend who chose golf over his family. Well, today I want to begin by telling you another story, this time about myself. I get very emotional telling it because this, along with the story I told you about my son and his fort, are two of the most powerful and insightful moments of my life.

"My friend said he wished he would have played less golf; well, at one time in my life, work was my golf. I think you have gotten that idea from what I've told you thus far. This story should bring everything I have said together and should really lead into what I have been getting at during this interview."

The student urged Bob to tell the story and assured him that being emotional was okay. Then Bob began.

"As you know, I have four children—three sons and one daughter. I have a special relationship with each of them, but a father's bond with his daughter is a particularly special one. I now have that bond with my daughter; but, when I was younger, I struggled with my priorities. This was overwhelmingly evident when my daughter was in second grade.

"She had this show at school where she and a friend were going to perform. She was so excited and she practiced for weeks. I still remember she was going to perform a song and dance to the song *Hot, Hot, Hot.* She had this cute little yellow outfit she was going to wear. For two weeks, she practiced with her friend, but she never let me see it. She wanted me to be surprised. She reminded me about it every day because she knew how busy I was at work, and that I had a tendency of missing things my kids did. I promised her I would be there.

"The performance was on a day I was teaching a class to a group of professionals. I decided to begin the class an hour early so I would have plenty of time to make it to the show. The class ended and I was going to have enough time to get there, but then there was a question and then another. I was stopped a few times on my way to my car and before I knew it I was strapped for time. I would be fine as long as I did not hit any traffic, but of course I did. As I was moving slowly in the traffic I kept saying to myself, 'I can't miss this! I can't do this to my daughter!' She was so excited!

"I got to the school and the parking lot was full. Whenever there is an event for high school-aged kids there is always plenty of parking, but when its elementary-aged kids everybody is there. Aunts, uncles, brothers, sisters, grandparents, parents, but me; I was not there yet. I finally found a spot in a field about a half mile away, and I sprinted to the school. I saw a side door so I tried to save time by using it, but it was locked. I went to the front and I heard the buzz inside. I walked in and saw on the program that she was fifth on the schedule, so I thought I was okay.

"I walked into the auditorium and there she was on stage. She looked right at me, smiled so big, and gave me a little wave. And then…she bowed. The crowd gave her a huge ovation. I realized I had just missed it. Then, just at that moment, my daughter looked at me again. She realized that, since I was standing at the door and she had not seen me before, I had missed her performance. The look on her face changed from that cute smile, to a look that has since been engrained on my mind, a look that I will never, ever forget."

Bob had struggled through the story and was very emotional in telling it, but he went on. "What I learned from that terrible experience of disappointing my one-and-only daughter was a pattern. I always pushed things to the limit. I always chose work over my family. Sure, I started the class an hour early, but I should have canceled it. By not canceling, I said the class was more important than my daughter. I chose success over my family, over what really mattered most. But I assure you, I have never made that mistake again."

After that story, Bob and the student sat in silence for a few minutes. Bob had tears in his eyes and the student had started to cry as well. The student was in awe of the story. He had never seen this side of Bob, but he realized this side of him was the reason he picked him to interview.

Then Bob broke the silence and said: "You told me, you decided to interview me because I have been the most influential person in your life. If that is the case, I am sure it is not because of my career success. I am not a millionaire. I have had my share of career successes, but none of that would matter without my family and without my relationship with God.

"The most important thing you need to do as you are preparing to graduate is figure out what matters most to you. Let me tell you now, that if your career is number one, something is wrong. If you let career success get in the way of relationships, then you will never be happy. I have told you about the seeds of success, but let me tell now about something else.

"I am sure you have seen the letters SOS on a lot of things I have written and prominently displayed in all of my favorite areas. SOS is a distress signal and something that will surely go off if you do not figure out what matters most in your life. That is what went off in my head when I saw the look of disappointment on my daughters face. SOS also stands for the seeds of success. But, more importantly, it is a question I ask myself regularly in my life. Will this lead to Success or Significance?

"That is the question you must ask yourself as you continue to grow as a person. Success is what you get on the way up. It's what we're always striving and achieving and reaching for. You get to a certain point and that kind of success does not really matter.

"Did you ever get something you really, really wanted and, when you got it, it was not as good as you thought? I have had that experience a lot. I told you about one of them. The award I worked so hard for just was not enough. That was because I was too concerned with success and not concerned enough about significance.

"It starts in our early lives. As children we cannot sleep on Christmas Eve. What's Santa Claus going to bring? And then Christmas morning comes, and it lasts five minutes. You open everything and then say, 'What's next?'

"That's what success is. Success is the ladder you climb on the way up. It's a ladder that leads to nowhere. You have heard the old saying, 'It's lonely at the top?' That's because that drive for worldly success is about ego and self-gratification. That's the trap. You have everything you thought you wanted and no one to share it with.

"It's really significance that we are seeking. It's not what we get, but rather what we leave behind that matters. So, I want to make sure before you get into that danger zone, before you start drawing SOS in the sand that you figure out what really matters most. It's about what you leave behind. It's answering God's call."

The student was speechless after hearing all of this, but he knew exactly what Bob was saying. He had been searching for something, and he now knew it was not success he was searching for and never was. He began to think about *The Last Lecture* and about the stories Bob had told him. He realized it was time for his life to begin.

He told Bob he was going to title his paper *Seeds of Success* and was going to use this paper as the stepping stone to the rest of his life. He would no longer be afraid of change or moving on. It was time for him to step up!

The student thanked Bob for his time and for all of the valuable insight he had given him. Bob said he looked forward to seeing how the paper turned out and that he would pray for the student as he began the new beginning of the rest of his life.

Then as the student was leaving Bob said one last thing to him and it was in the form of a poem. He said:

"I have a premonition that soars on silvered wings,
A dream of your accomplishments
and other wondrous things,
I do not know beneath what sky
Or where you'll challenge fate,
I only know it will be high,
I only know you will be GREAT!"[11]

"That is my wish for you," Bob said. "Now let's go for it!"

---

11 Anonymous

SEEDS TO PLANT

Be on the lookout for the SOS distress signal!

Decide what matters most. God and Family should be the answer.

Success or Significance? What will you choose?

Seeds of Success

7

The Final Paper

The student had concluded the interviews and began writing his paper. He had taken a plethora of notes in the interviews, which he was sorting through and recorded. He had developed a vision for the paper. He wanted to include a lot of the information he received from the interviews and throw in a couple of the stories. But he also wanted to put some other examples in it from his own life.

He entitled the paper, *Seeds of Success*, as he said he would. The first paragraph of the paper went like this:

"Everyone has dreams and goals for their life. But in order to find success, they must first plant the seeds. The seeds of success can be different for each person, but there are some that are essential and they will be detailed in this paper."

The student went on to detail some of the key insights on leadership and success he had learned in his interviews, beginning by discussing some basic fundamentals of leadership. He wrote about teamwork and the magical season when he learned about playing as a team, and how much more success one could have when they realized they were part of a team. He wrote about his experience as point guard on the team, and how that experience helped him in other leadership roles he held over the years. He used the example of running for junior class president in high school because he knew he was the most qualified and could lead the class through a tough year.

Then he wrote about some of the seeds his teacher had planted. He told how leadership is really just about influence. Negative influences are all around and people have to be able to weed them out and focus on the positive. His former youth minister talked about how people tend to focus on those negative influences even though it is the positive ones that are the most powerful. The student used the story of the girl who asked him to be her Confirmation sponsor to illustrate that point.

He highlighted everything discussed in the interviews, saving a few points for the end of the paper. He spent three pages on the three seeds that went so closely together. Forgiveness, change, and overcoming the past were his three favorite seeds. He saw them as the most important and the perfect way to lead into his conclusion.

He used Bob's stories to demonstrate his points on each of the seeds, realizing the stories were far better than anything he could write. He did add something to the part about change. He used a quote from *Rocky IV*, when

Rocky speaks to the crowd of Russians after defeating Ivan Drago. He said, "If I can change, and you can change, everybody can change." Rocky must have been a genius because he got it exactly right. Everyone is capable of change. Rocky walked into the ring to boos and threats, but came out with the love and support of a nation. Drago walked in hearing cheers, but left hearing boos. That was a lot of change in a short period of time, but it shows that people can change. The reference may have been a stretch, but the student jumped at any opportunity to include Rocky in a paper.

He had now written eighty-five percent of the paper. All that was left was the conclusion. This was his chance to talk about what had been the most interesting insight he had gotten from the interviews. He hesitated at first because the assignment was to explain the keys to success. Should he deviate from the assignment and talk about what really mattered?

He thought for a long time about where he was in his life before this assignment. He was lost. Searching. Maybe it was the same funk every college student goes through before graduation. Or, perhaps it had been more. Maybe this assignment was not given by a professor? Maybe it was a sign from God? A gift from God? A chance to get his life on track and finally figure out what mattered most? After all of this thinking, a little voice finally said, "Go for it!" And he did just that. The conclusion of the paper read like this:

> "This assignment was supposed to yield great insight on the keys to success, and it did just that for me. What exactly is success? I have found, in

these interviews, that success is really just what people look for on the way up. When they are on their way, they see possessions as important. They want to be successful in their careers. They also want to have successful lives, but as they are on their way up, careers and life are one in the same.

"As a young man on the verge of graduating from college and heading out into the real world, one would think that success as I have defined it would be important to me. I am on my way up.

"The difference, though, between me and other people my age, is that I have already realized what matters most. This assignment has helped me with that. Success is not what is important. The people that are only concerned with success are the ones who leave nothing behind. They are the ones that neglect the people they love most. They are the ones who never put God first in their lives.

"I titled this paper, *Seeds of Success.* I believe that is an appropriate title because everything I have discussed thus far has been the seeds that need to be planted in order to live a successful life. But I could have entitled the paper, *Success or Significance?* That is what I have gained from this assignment.

"Significance is being concerned with what one leaves behind and, although I am at the beginning of my life, I know that is true. All of the seeds I have written about are really summed up with one word. That being significance. No amount of success in the world can trump significance.

"The assignment was to find out the keys to success. My key to success is to find out what matters most and lead a life of significance. This is what I will do, and I pray others will follow. **Success is not a destination, it is a journey. But really, it is not about success at all, it is about significance.** My question for everyone is this: Success or Significance? What will you choose?"

The student turned in the paper and waited anxiously for the next class when they would be returned. He had never been so concerned with a grade before. The professor held a discussion on the topic before returning the papers. She used a few examples from his paper. He thought that was a good sign.

Then she began handing back the papers. When she came to him, he closed his eyes as she placed the paper on his desk. He turned it over and saw a big "A." He was ecstatic, but then he noticed the words "see me" written by the grade. He was still happy about the grade, but he wondered what this was about. He had seen these words before, and they had never been good news.

When class ended, he approached the professor to see what the problem was. He said, "You wanted to see me?"

"I did," the professor said. "First, I just wanted to say this was one of the best papers I have ever read. Some of what you said is still engrained on my mind, and I may actually change the assignment to something about finding what matters most. The only question I had was about your interviews. You conducted four interviews, but on your bibliography, you only listed one person? I assume that was just a mistake?"

The student then explained why this was the case. "It was actually not a mistake. You see, when you explained the assignment, I thought long and hard about whom I would interview. When I broke down the different areas of my life, I realized that the same person had been the most influential in each area. And that person was also the most successful person I knew. To be completely honest, there is not one area of my life where he is not the most influential person."

Success is not a destination, it is a journey. But really, it is not about success at all, it is about significance.

The teacher was surprised by all of this, but let the student go on with the "A." She had never actually said it had to be different people, but it never occurred to her that someone would interview just one person four times.

The student thought nothing of it and left the classroom on a high. He had just had his best college experience. This assignment had changed his life, and he even got an "A." That was something new to him.

══ 8 ══

A New Beginning

With the end of the assignment came the end of the semester. The student was still excited about his "A," but he decided to wait until he saw Bob (coach, teacher, youth minister) to tell him about the grade.

It is funny how sometimes one simple thing, or in this case an assignment, can change a person's life. That was the case for the student. While working on the assignment, he got to really thinking about what he wanted to do with his life. He knew he wanted his life to mean something, not just to himself, but to other people as well.

Not only did the assignment make the student think about his future, it also changed his outlook on life. It got him out of that funk. He knew people his age and in his position were usually scared and sometimes clueless, but he had felt like it was worse for him. Now he was out of that funk. He began to realize that while he was in that funk, he did not treat the people close to him well. He changed that right away. He knew what mattered most now.

So what did the student decide to do? What was his career choice? That is what everyone wants to know when a person is getting ready to graduate. The student now knew that, but he wanted to tell Bob the news first.

Graduation was finally here for the student. He attended the Baccalaureate Mass the night before and, of course, Bob was there. After the Mass and all the pictures that come with being in a cap and gown, the student took Bob aside to tell him about his "A."

When they were alone, the student handed Bob his final paper. Bob slowly looked at it and then congratulated him. Then he began to skim through the paper, and he was extremely interested. He continued to scan the paper until he came to the conclusion. The student could then hear Bob reading in a whisper. The whisper then became louder and louder. When he got to the final challenge, he read aloud in an emotional and proud voice.

"Success is not a destination, it is a journey. But really it is not about success at all, it is about significance. My question for everyone is this: Success or Significance? What will you choose?"

Bob was happy that the student had gotten it right. He then said to the student, "So what do you choose, success or significance?"

The student said, "I have been thinking about that since I talked to you last and throughout this assignment. I am on the way up, so maybe I should choose success. But that is not what I choose. I choose to be like YOU. That is my greatest insight from this assignment. By choosing to be like you, I am choosing significance because you have led a significant life, and I can only hope to be half the man you are."

Bob was surprised by this answer, and he continued to tear up. The student went on, "I do not mean I want to be like you in a small way. That is what I want to do with my life. In listening to your stories and in writing this paper, I had a few different "ah-ha moments." I had one when you passed along the video of *The Last Lecture.* I had one during each interview. The whole project was one big "ah-ha moment," and I realized that for as long as I can remember I wanted to be just like you. I guess I forgot that over the past couple years. But now I want to start being like you."

Bob was touched by all of this. He then said, "So what did your professor think about you interviewing me for each part?"

"She was not too sure about it," the student said. "She thought it was a mistake and when I told her it wasn't, she didn't really understand. I guess she did not have a hero growing up. You are my hero, and you always have been. Thanks for everything you have done for me. I am glad I got to share all of this with you."

Bob then hugged the student and told him he was proud of him.

During the hug the student said, "I love you, Dad." His father, Bob, replied, "I love you too, son."

Epilogue

The story that has been told is quite a powerful one. As said in the introduction, this book has been a long time coming. One of the reasons for it not happening faster was because of not knowing how to best format the book.

There were a plethora of ideas that we wanted to pass on, but how? After going through all the different ways the book could be written, it became obvious how it should be done. The book is about leadership, success, and, most of all, significance. With all the references to significance, what better way to format it then to make it a conversation between a father and son.

A while back we were speaking to a group of about fifty men. We asked them the question, "who is your spiritual role model and essentially who has been your hero in your life?" We got a lot of answers, but it took about ten different people until someone said their father. After this, we asked how many people chose to write down their father. Only two people raised their hands.

What a shame that is. Parents should be their children's heroes. They should be good role models for them. But the truth is this is simply not the case most of the time. Life gets in the way. Work gets in the way. Work is too often considered to be life.

It is possible to have a successful career and spend ample time with your family, but you must remember what matters most! What are your priorities? Do you want to have a successful career? Do you want money? What if you could have those things, but you had to sacrifice your relationship with your children? With your spouse? What if your children grow up and they are asked who in their lives had the biggest influence, and they do not answer by saying you. That would be a tragedy.

You need to be on the lookout for distress signals in your life. Look for that SOS that was talked about in the book. Remember, if you are traveling down the path toward success and not seeking significance, then you must CHANGE! The man in the book who was being interviewed faced an SOS in his life, and he changed. He chose the road of significance and that is why his son wanted to be just like him.

It is time we ask ourselves some hard questions about the long-term effectiveness of the message in this book. In the parable of the sower in Matthew 13:3-23, the seed was sown but not all the seed endured until the crop was produced. The seed was sown, but with different results:

1. *Some fell by the wayside and the birds got them.*

Some of you will hear this warning, but it never gets down into your understanding; therefore, there is no positive response. Before you have a chance to believe, other things distract you or you begin reading the next self-help book that you won't implement.

2. *Some fell on stony ground and had shallow roots.*

If you are in this group, you hear the message, but before you truly, deeply understand the whole message, you let your emotions begin to run away with you. This group's highs are higher than anyone else, and their lows are lower than anyone else. Because the true understanding is set aside by your shallow response on the emotional level, when hard times come, there is nothing there to keep the faith. Even though you appear to have a genuine experience, the hard times prove something to be lacking, as you pull back from the fervent zeal you had at the beginning of the change process.

3. Some sprung up and the thorns choked them out.

In this group, you seem to have a genuine response. You hear the message, and it appears that you have every intention to follow through with your decision. Somewhere along the way, however, the day-to-day pressures of simply living begin to drain away the intensity of your commitment. As much as you want to do what you committed to do, something more important is always demanding your attention. Eventually, your desire loses out to neglect. The end result is the same as the first two responses. The only difference is that it takes a little longer before the message becomes ineffective.

4. Some fell on good soil and brought forth one hundred, sixty, and thirty fold.

When this message finds a hungry, yearning heart that sincerely responds to it, your understanding explodes. The heart of the true believer resonates with the opportunity to give away what you have just received. The reality of your newfound growth compels you to share the message with all of your friends and family. You become living witnesses of what you have experienced. As a result, others discover the same possibilities. In fact, most people see the responses of categories two and three along with four and believe that all who show initial excitement will somehow follow through with their commitment. But we know from the parable this simply is not true. By sowing the seed and simply leaving it, the harvest will not be three out of four, but rather one out of four.

Simple mathematics tells us, if we think we are seventy-five percent effective when we are really only twenty-five percent effective, we have the feeling of winning; but we are, in fact, losing. Darkness is quite happy with the status quo. If this is even a fairly accurate representation of our effectiveness, then something quite different is required if we are ever to make major inroads into the strongholds that enslave us. Number two was due to misplaced over-enthusiasm. Change isn't easy. When difficulties arose, there wasn't a deep enough understanding for the initial commitment to sustain the life of the seed. The seed sown was attacked by thorns (number three), indicating the importance of the decision to receive the message simply gets shoved aside by the many demands of life. Hopefully, this book provided you with some serious insights. As you learned, insight precedes change, but insight itself isn't change.

The time is now for you to begin planting your own seeds of success and realizing that all you must do to be truly successful is lead a life of significance. This book provided you with some seeds you can plant in order to do just that. You may discover, though, that you have a few weeds to pull in some of your relationships. You may also find that the new YOU is not instantly accepted and some of your new seeds will fall on rocky ground. Be patient and stay the course. Use the ideas and the stories that went with them to guide you in your journey, just as the student did.

The reality is that the student was not searching for help with a paper. He was not looking for an "A." He was just looking for guidance. He found that guidance. Actually, I think I can stop speaking in the third person now. I found that guidance. I have found more guidance everyday when I talk to my dad and mom.

As I have grown up, I have tagged along with my dad everywhere. I have learned from him. The most valuable information I have learned thus far in my life has not come in a classroom. It has come from my heroes, my parents. I pray that more people can have that same experience. But it starts with YOU!

If you are at a place in your life where you have achieved a certain level of what you would call success, but are still not happy, then you need to find significance. It is not too late!

If you are in the middle of your life, maybe you are married and have a child, but you are struggling to balance your work and your family, remember that relationships bring significance. Be a successful spouse and parent. The career success will come. And if it doesn't, then at least you will have a family who loves, respects, and looks up to you.

And finally, if you are where I am in life, just beginning your career, then do not let yourself ever be in one of those previous statements. Learn, as I did, from the stories in this book. Decide right now, that you are going to live that life of significance!

If you lead that life, then you will truly find out the meaning of the word success! And I promise you, there will be no amount of money that can top that.
—Billy Moyer

Bill and Billy Moyer after speaking to a group in 1995.

The teacher and the student at St. Edward's University graduation.

Acknowledgements

Bill Moyer—I would like to express whole-hearted gratitude for all who have touched my life including:

Paul J. Meyer, for opening up a whole new world to me and for teaching me that whatever you vividly imagine, ardently desire, sincerely believe, and enthusiastically act upon… must inevitably come to pass!

Tammie, my assistant, for all of the hard work in helping with this book and all of the Seeds of Success programs.

Dawn James, my long-time former assistant, for helping to design and create the original Seeds of Success material.

Chris, for allowing me to practice on you as most parents do on their firstborn.

Brian, for sharing my passion for teaching and coaching.

Amber, for sharing my passion for Christian service and challenging me to always reach for the stars.

Billy, for being the driving force in making this book happen, but especially for the times we had together doing retreats and speaking.

My late parents, Bill and Ann Moyer, for planting the seeds of success in me.

Lastly, and most importantly, my wife of over thirty years Rose, for always challenging me to be a better person and for inspiring me each and every day with your unconditional love and devotion to the family.

Acknowledgements

Billy Moyer—I would like to express whole-hearted praise and gratitude to:

Shane, my best friend of over seventeen years, thanks for always being there for me.

Heather, for motivating and inspiring me in ways I could never fully explain.

All of the great teachers I have had in my life, including Sister Kenneth, Mrs. Barnes, Mrs. Lichte, Mrs. Stryker, Mrs. Glover, and Billy Earnest.

Paul J. Meyer, you are one of my dads mentors, therefore you are one of mine. I will always remember that "if you are not making the progress you would like to be making and are capable of making, it is simply because your goals are not clearly defined."

Chris, for being my AC buddy and for being a great older brother.

Brian, for providing a great example of hard work to me as my older brother and for taking me on our five-thousand-miles-of-dreams road trip.

Martin, for being the best brother-in-law a guy could ask for, and most of all for being a great friend.

Amber, for always being there for me and for inspiring me to try and be half of the amazing person you are.

Grace, for being the best goddaughter ever!

Mom, for being such a fun and loving person to me and for putting up with me for all these years. I love you!

And last, but certainly not least, Dad. Thank you for allowing me to be a part of this book. I am proud to be your son.

About the Authors

Bill Moyer is the Executive Director of the National Fellowship of Catholic Men. He also serves as the Chief Spiritual Officer of SOS Leadership Institute. He has invested over twenty-five years defining "What Matters Most" as a focus, rather than a question, in this ever-changing world. This focus generates organizational clarity and builds a results-based culture.

Bill has been a successful entrepreneur, building two startup companies, and has served as a senior executive in the Paul J. Meyer Companies including Leadership Management International, Success Motivation Institute, Church Growth International, My-Tyme, Inc, and Creative Education Institute. He has served as a turnaround specialist for four companies and has been an executive coach to many corporate CEO's and executives.

Bill has spoken to business leaders in thirty-five countries and forty-nine states on effective leadership and has authored more than fifty articles in business publications. He is regarded as an expert in "What Matters Most" for business leaders...achieving long-term, sustainable growth through ethical leadership.

Bill resides in Waco, TX, with his wife Rose of over thirty years. He has four children and three grandchildren.

Billy Moyer is the co-founder and President of SOS Leadership Institute, an organization that focuses on developing the heart and soul of the Christian leader.

He has a Bachelor's degree in Communication from St. Edward's University in Austin, Texas. He has written and has had published more than twenty articles. He is also an accomplished public speaker and has spoken to groups of all sizes on subjects such as teamwork, self-image, ministry, and goal setting.

He has been around the leadership development industry all of his life where he has learned about the over-whelming power of goal setting and the importance of time management. Most of all he has learned from his father and co-founder of SOS Leadership, the concept of "What Matters Most" in business and in life. He realizes the remarkable importance of living a life of significance. Together, Billy and his father have put on over one-hundred-fifty retreats and have spoken at a plethora of other workshops and conventions.

Billy is pursuing a Master's Degree in Organizational Leadership at Gonzaga University. He resides in Austin, Texas.

SOS Leadership Institute

SOS Leadership Institute out of Waco and Austin, Texas, is an organization primarily concerned with developing the heart and soul of Christian leaders. SOS Leadership serves as a wake-up call for struggling leaders in this fast-paced, money-hungry world.

Why SOS? When someone is in trouble they send out distress signals, which get in the way of their abilities as leaders. The most common distress signal is SOS. But that is not the only reason. SOS also stands for *Seeds of Success*.

Most importantly, SOS stands for Success or Significance? SOS Leadership firmly believes that success is not possible without living a life of significance. To do this one must realize what matters most in their lives.

SOS Leadership provides training, coaching, keynote speaking, workshops, and retreats for people who want to focus on personal leadership, which is determining what matters most.

For more information about SOS Leadership Institute visit www.sosleadership.com or email info@sosleadership.com.

National Fellowship of Catholic Men

The National Fellowship of Catholic Men (NFCM) is a national organization established in 2001 and serves regional and local Catholic men's fellowships and Catholic men's faith groups by providing resources, leadership training, and communications.

Specifically, the NFCM was formed to help Catholic men grow in their spiritual lives, their marriages and families, their jobs, and every aspect of their lives. A significant contributor to this growth will be the ongoing support of other deeply committed Christian men. For more information about NFCM or to make a donation please visit www.NFCMusa.org.

Author Contact Information

You can contact the authors, Bill Moyer or Billy Moyer,
at: info@sosleadership.com
View the *SOS Leadership* company and
book website at: www.sosleadership.com